AF557845

RSS
Building India through *sewa*

RSS

Building India through *sewa*

Sudhanshu Mittal

HAR-ANAND
PUBLICATIONS PVT LTD

Editorial Support: Deepanjali Bhaas

Published by Ashok Gosain and Ashish Gosain for:
HAR-ANAND PUBLICATIONS PVT LTD
E-49/3, Okhla Industrial Area, Phase-II, New Delhi-110020
Tel: 41603490
E-mail: info@haranandbooks.com/haranand@rediffmail.com
Shop online at: www.haranandbooks.com

Printed in India at Vinayak Offset.

Preface

Over the last four decades, I have been a Swayam Sevak of the RSS. I have seen RSS's core ideology of *sewa*—service for others—preached and in action. But I have also come to witness that many Indians, especially in urban areas, are shy to acknowledge RSS's contributions and consider it a right-wing Hindu fundamental organization; supporting or even investing in parsing the fact from fiction around the RSS is looked down upon. In the midst of inflammatory statements from so-called RSS leaders and news attributing communal violence to the RSS, one finds oneself worrying about how any implicit or tacit support of RSS can be viewed by friends and acquaintances.

I wrote this book to differentiate between the fact and the fiction that is at the heart of the debate on the RSS, and to attempt to clarify RSS's contribution to and position in Indian society. Undoubtedly, there are factions that will cause imbalance or incite violence in the name of the RSS—but I have seen that this is neither the position of the organization nor is it supported by its leadership in actions or messaging. I have strived to put together a book that explores this tension objectively, and lends light to RSS's history, ideology and policies, and their subsequent impact on the nation.

I hope you all enjoy reading and sharing this book as much as I have enjoyed putting it together.

SUDHANSHU MITTAL

Acknowledgement

I owe this book to many more people than I can note—from the *sewaks* and leaders of the RSS, to my friends and family who have supported me at every turning point in my life, regardless of which direction life has taken me. I would like to take a brief moment to acknowledge some people in particular, without whom this book would remain indefinitely a mere thought within the confines of my mind.

My gratitude to the *Pracharaks* of RSS. Watching many of them dedicate their lives to the service of their communities while asking for little in return has greatly moved and inspired me, and is the driving force for this book. I only hope I have been able to shed light on their unwavering commitment to our great nation.

A big thank you to Shri Dattatreya Hosable ji, the present Sah-Sarakayavah (Joint General-Secretary) of RSS, whom I have known for nearly four decades and view as my role model and guide. Often, I have sparred with him on ideological and organizational issues surrounding the RSS. Our lengthy discussions have been invaluable in aiding my journey to understand the history and values of the RSS. Thank you Hosable ji for inspiring me to strive relentlessly towards a better future, put service above self, and dedicate myself to the betterment of my fellow Indians. Without his encouragement, I would have never put paper to pen to share my thoughts on the RSS with the broader world.

The acknowledgements would not be complete without mentioning Shri Krishan Gopal ji. I first met Gopal ji during 2009 Lok Sabha elections, when he was RSS's *Shetriya Pracharak* for the North-East and I was in-charge of elections in the North-East for the BJP. Despite being born and brought up in western Uttar Pradesh, he moved to remote parts of the North-East and spent more than nine years devoted to uplifting tribal North-Eastern communities. His work to integrate the most remote parts of our nation into the centerfold reflects to me the core ideology and commitment to the community that is core to the RSS mission and identity. I consider myself fortunate to have had the opportunity to interact with him closely over the last few years.

My thoughts stray to the late Shri Pramod Mahajan, my political mentor and friend. Despite the years, his animated and passionate recounting of RSS's *Sanganthan Shastra* and his clarity of vision, awe-inspiring political acumen, and sharp wit remain as vivid in my memory as if we last spoke just yesterday. I owe my political and social journey to the lessons I learnt from him, and my heart swells with pride to see many of his interpretations and insights on RSS's organizational skills being adopted by the BJP today.

I am grateful to my wife, Dr. Rubina Mittal, without whom this book would have never seen the light of the day. Not only is Rubina a Professor of Applied Mathematics at Delhi University, she is also the de-facto **Editor** of this book. Any semblance of order in this book can be attributed to her sharp edits and commitment to reading my manuscript again and again, till it took the crisp form it has today. Rubina, you are a grounding force in my life; thank you for always encouraging me to pour my passion into words.

A special thank you to Deepanjali Bhas for putting in weeks of work to help me research the material for the book and provide editorial support; my father for inspiring me with his tireless work ethics and for introducing me to RSS *shakhas* at a young age; my late mother for supporting me unconditionally in all my endeavors; my children, Devansh and Devika, for being in my life and inspiring me to be my best self.

Last but certainly not least, thank you to my publisher Shri Narendra Kumar Ji of Har-Anand Publications. I think I have spent more time discussing Indian politics with him than anyone else, and am always bowled over by his infinite curiosity and vast knowledge around global and Indian affairs. Thank you for pushing me to write a book that you will be proud to publish.

Contents

Introduction 11

1. Origin and History of RSS 23
2. Unique Structural Organisation 50
3. Sewa Karya—The Heart and Soul of RSS 61
4. RSS Chronology with Major Indian Political and Social Events 93
5. RSS and Independence of India 106
6. Sangh and Generational Change 124
7. RSS and Global Challenges 135
8. RSS and Call for Justice in Ram Janmabhoomi 146

Appendix 160

Introduction

"Only a piece of land cannot be called 'Nation'. A nation is created where people of one thought, one culture and one tradition live together since ancient times. Because of exactly the above reasons, 'Hindustan' is the name given to our country and this is a country of the Hindus."

Dr Keshav Baliram Hedgewar,
Founder of Rashtriya Swayamsevak Sangh

Rashtriya Swayam Sevak Sangh (RSS) is one of the most unique organizations in the world. With no formal membership it has survived for nearly a century and grown, despite facing restrictions from past governments, as well as continuous misrepresentation in the Indian and international media. Seeing India through a volatile Independence and tragic Partition in 1947, RSS has evolved over the decades with a mission to stand for a confident nation and work tirelessly and selflessly for all Indians irrespective of socio-economic or religious affiliation. With 58,967 Shakhas (the fundamental unit of RSS activity) at 37,190 places, in addition to weekly gatherings at 16,405 places and monthly meetings at 7,976 places (as on March 2018), informal estimates point to a membership of over 9 million. The numbers are more if one considers persons who don't attend shakhas but contribute to and participate in activities. Affiliate organizations touch on every aspect of human life—schools, student and trade associations, and outreach to vulnerable tribal communities. The RSS's Vidya Bharti Schools across India are the largest network of private schools in the country, numbering 12,000 with over 32 lakh students enrolled. The innovative Ekal Vidyalaya or one-teacher schools in remote tribal areas of India ensure children in such regions are not deprived of education. The RSS has a truly pan-India nationalist footprint and is the largest non-governmental organization in the world that functions not through donations but through voluntary contributions of members or anyone who is interested.

And yet, the RSS, that so positively impacts the lives of millions of people, has not got its due in the public domain managed by media; it has instead, become the favourite punching bag of a biased media since Independence that has done little to report its hard work on the ground. Despite espousing a philosophy of the ancient Upanishads, "Vasudhaiva Kutumbakam" (The World is One Family), the RSS has been needlessly vilified.

BRITISH COLONIZATION OF THE INDIAN MIND

India is the only large non-English speaking country in the world where the preferred language of education and communication for upward mobility is a foreign language—English. No other country, whether in Europe or Asia, chooses to speak in a language other than its own.

This has its roots in a deeply entrenched inferiority complex that was brought about by the British Raj. The British colonisers of India could see that if the Hindus could withstand, for close to 1000 years, Islamic invasions, repression and torture and still stay true to their faith, physical force alone would not be of much use to subdue them. So the British went a step further and worked at colonizing the minds of educated Indians. The British aimed at creating the "brown sahibs," and a Western-inspired elite was then formed through the English education system which produced the administrative force the British needed. Members of this elite class scorned their own cultural roots and with them in positions of power in policy making, ensured the unique cultural identity of India would be steadily eroded, just as the British wanted, even after Independence.

RSS Founder Dr Hedgewar ji could see this happening in the 1920s. Unfortunately, this Westernised elite class with its contempt for its own heritage (even as the West looks to India's Hindu traditions for guidance) still persists, creating conflicts between the majority of Indians who are rooted in their cultural traditions and identity of over 10,000 years, and the foreign ideas of this elite.

I am a proud member of the RSS and believe that any organization should be evaluated by its deeds and not its professed philosophy (or worse, philosophy misrepresented by the media). It is in the domain of work through Sewa (service) that RSS's commitment rings true. In the devastating Kerala Floods of August 2018, RSS's Sewa Bharti volunteers were the first to hit the ground and rescue a large number of people, risking their own lives and eventually leading to the death of two swayamsevaks. One wonders what could make simple, ordinary citizens go out to save people risking their own lives. For the RSS worker, though, that is his calling, for which he has trained for years; to serve the needy in all ways possible while not craving publicity. The RSS is a mission that truly unifies India.

But it is the humility of the RSS—the decision not to react when attacked by the media or politicians or to publicise its work—that has led people to think of the organization as the many things that it is not. When RSS Sarsangchalak (chief) Dr Mohan Bhagwat ji said in September 2018 during the RSS Lecture Series, that there can be no Hindu Rashtra or Hindutva without Muslims, it created a flurry in the media. Shri Bhagwat ji's statement was a departure from the views of the second Sarsangchalak Shri Guruji Golwalkar (in his famous 1966 book A Bunch of Thoughts). The media's confusion was not surprising, since their views were coloured by past journalistic reportage and they had not cared to learn more about the RSS. But those who know the Sangh know that it has always been inclusive, ideologically and in practice, and this can be seen in every single activity that the RSS is involved in. The RSS is not a static organization but a dynamic one that responds to the current needs of society. Like Shri Bhagwat ji said, what was relevant in 1925 or 1947 may not be relevant today.

Let us, for instance, look at the Indian National Congress. The INC was the torchbearer of the Indian freedom movement in the early 20th century but if anybody were to evaluate the Congress party today, can they say this party is what the INC was during the Freedom Movement, the party of Annie Besant, Lokmanya Tilak, Mahatma Gandhi? No, they cannot, because today the party has degenerated.

THE NATIONAL FLAG WAS KEPT PRISONER UNTIL 2002!

It is often said that the RSS did not hoist the national flag on its premises when that is not true. On 15 August 1947, the national flag was first hoisted at the RSS headquarters and again on 26 January 1950. So the canard goes that the RSS did not hoist the national flag since then. Does anyone care to note that this was because the first government of Independent India had made laws that allowed only government buildings to hoist the national flag? The National Flag was kept prisoner by the Congress party! It was only after 2002 when a historic Supreme Court judgment declared hoisting the Tricolour a Fundamental Right of citizens of India, that it became free.

From 26 January 2002, when the New Flag Code 2002 replaced the old one, all citizens were given the right to hoist the national flag whereas previously only government buildings were allowed to do so. The Tiranga was seen flying at the RSS premises in 2002, when it was hoisted at the Nagpur headquarters and Smruti Bhawan, the building that houses the memorials of its founder Hedgewar and Guru Golwalkar.

With regard to the saffron flag (Bhagwa Dhwaj) of the RSS that marks India's ancient cultural heritage, it has seen enough criticism and is still called sectarian and communal. But Dr BR Ambedkar too held the view that the saffron flag should be adopted as the National Flag and Sanskrit should become the national language. This was pointed out by RSS Sarsangchalak Shri Bhagwat ji in 2016.

THE FUNDAMENTAL IS SEWA

Though it is statements by RSS leaders that often hit the headlines, it is important to point out that the FUNDAMENTAL PHILOSPHY OF THE RSS IS SEWA—service. Sangh believes everyone who is culturally Hindu has benefitted from society and has a duty to give back in turn. It functions on the credo of Vyakti nirman (building an individual's character) and through it samaaj nirman (building the character of a society). Sewa is in keeping with the ancient Hindu philosophy of service to all without expectation of reward or recognition.

- RSS was started by Dr Keshav Balirao Hedgewar, a medical doctor and staunch nationalist in 1925 along with 17 persons in his simple home in Nagpur, Maharashtra. He was the first sarsangchalak (head of the RSS) and was also an active Congressman. (That the Indian National Congress (INC) party of today is NOT the party it was in the 20th Century is perhaps not appreciable to many. It is important to note the facts of history that INC was the only representative national party advocating for independence from the British and had a mix of members in it of varying ideologies like socialists, Hindu cultural revivalists and those leaning to the economic right.)
- In the early days of the RSS, with increasing separatist activity from Muslims and riots in several areas in India in which large numbers of Hindus were brutally murdered, raped and forcibly converted to Islam (like the Moplah riots in Malabar, Kerala), the aim before the RSS was to organize a Hindu society that had been mostly divided by caste and was unable to withstand the onslaught of the more organized Muslims.
- The shakha was the focus, a meeting place where young men at village, district or state level could meet and be trained in the martial arts, gain an understanding of India's Hindu spiritual heritage and to work towards freeing India from British rule. A shakha is a daily gathering of swayamsevaks (volunteers) across age groups at a meeting place or ground for an hour. Daily routine programs include physical exercises, singing patriotic songs, group discussions on varied range of subjects and a prayer for our motherland. It was these shakhas that enabled

the mobilization of hundreds of thousands of swayamsevaks who were able to help millions of refugees from West Punjab and East Bengal who had flooded into India in the horrendous aftermath of Partition and the creation of Pakistan as a nation for Muslims in 1947.

- The transition in RSS from a Shakha orientation to the focus on Sewa happened over the decades after Independence to address the problems faced by Indians at the grassroots on account of poverty and social discrimination. This marks a classic case of changeability in an organization viz. society where it is responsive to people's needs. Affiliate organizations have been constituted as and when there is a need felt from communities. These organizations function as independent bodies in themselves. A good example of a neglected community need that the RSS responded to a few years after Independence is the Akhil Bharatiya Vanvasi Kalyan Ashram that was formed in 1952 to serve vulnerable tribals who number an estimated 104 million in India. This affiliate organization was formed to prevent tribal exploitation on economic and hence religious grounds by vested interests especially conversion to religions like Christianity whose missionaries were (and still are) active in these regions and whose community service is an inducement done to convert the communities to Christianity.
- The largest activity of RSS—Sewa—is NOT in the public domain. The urban elite see RSS as an excellent disaster management organization saving lives of millions during natural disasters and emergencies. When, in fact, it is an organization that functions non-stop, 24/7, and 365 days a year. The RSS is merged with Indian society. It is the society that contributes to this organization and the members work with society. It is a unique organisational model.

RSS AND INDIAN FREEDOM STRUGGLE

India was Always one Nation

"It was the wily foreigner, the Britisher, who to achieve his ulterior imperialistic motives, set afloat all such mischievous notions among our people so that the sense of patriotism and duty towards the integrated personality of our motherland was corroded. He carried on an insidious propaganda that we were never one nation, that we were never the children of the soil, but mere upstarts having no better claims than the foreign hordes of the Muslims or the British over this country. The misfortune is that the so-called educated of this land were taken in by this ruse.

But the fact is, long before the West had learnt to eat roast meat instead of raw, we were one nation, with one motherland.... Long ago our forefathers sang: 'The land to the north of the oceans and south of the Himalayas is called Bharatavarsha, and Bharatis are her children.'"

"Shri Guruji Golwakar in a Bunch of Thoughts (1966)"
RSS and Indian Freedom Struggle

The RSS in its inception in 1925, defined itself as a nationalist organisation dedicated to the motherland and its freedom. This was quite unlike the Indian National Congress which only in 1929, 44 years after it was started, demanded Poorna Swarajya (full independence). This, of course nobody bothers to note, but instead lies are spread over the decades that RSS did not take part in the freedom struggle. The RSS Pledge (Pratigya) right form its start until Independence used to contain the words "Desh ko Swatantra Kar" ("Free the country"). The RSS Founder Dr Shri Hedgewar ji, was a member of the INC, an active participant in the Satyagraha and the Quit India Movement led by Gandhi ji, and was imprisoned twice. Hundreds of RSS swayamsevaks were involved in the freedom struggle and gave up their lives.

In fact, it may surprise many to know that much before the demand for Full Independence was raised by INC, it was Doctor

Hedgewar ji who was part of a movement in INC which, in fact, first made such a resolution. As a member of INC, Doctor Hedgewar had formed the Nagpur National Union with some friends. As in charge of the volunteer force for the All India Congress Committee session in Nagpur in 1920, the Nagpur National Union submitted a resolution to the Subjects Committee of INC and demanded the Congress declare "complete independence as it sole objective." The resolution was rejected by the Steering Committee, but it is pertinent to note that Dr Hedgewar raised the call for complete Independence for India nearly 10 years before the INC did!

It would be enlightening for the reader to know of the immense contribution of the swayamsevaks during the Quit India Movement when, after the arrest of all the top INC leaders by the British, the Congress cadre did not know what to do and it was the swayamsevaks that kept the movement going strong underground, offering safety and security to Congress leaders in hiding as well. The work of the RSS was appreciated by Gandhi ji who was impressed by the totally egalitarian functioning of the Sangh where Swayamsevaks did not even knew each other's caste.

This book describes how the commitment and dedication to the Independence movement by swayamsevaks has gone unsung as they chose not to publicise their work.

THE NATION IS ALWAYS FIRST

In a country as diverse as India, contentious issues are naturally, aplenty. For a young democracy like India, that critical areas in gender equity that affect the lives, dignity and safety of women remain untouched only because they are encased in religions that are non-Hindu, is a great shame. RSS has never had double standards on such issues like Triple Talaq, Nikah Halala in Islam that have come to the forefront in recent years in India through a slew of complaints from aggrieved women and a clear Supreme Court judgment thereof. The Sangh has also been active earlier in fighting for reform in Hindu society like Abolition of Sati and enabling legal recourse for married women harassed on account of dowry.

A Uniform Civil Code (UCC), as enshrined in the Directive Principles of State Policy in the Constitution of India, is a demand that the RSS stands by because of the "rightness" of it. It has always been clear for RSS that one country must have one set of laws and there can be no separate laws in the name of minority appeasement as is currently the practice in India. It is noteworthy that the RSS has never batted for a Hindu Civil Code and hence calling RSS dogmatic is unfair and wrong. It is a progressive, reformist organisation and its stand against appeasement of minorities is clearly in favour of gender equity as women have had to bear the brunt of religious personal laws. RSS believes it is the politics of appeasement practised by the Congress and other such parties that has actually prevented gender equity in India while the media has stood by as a silent spectator for the last 70 years. The policy of RSS is on the lines of what one of the distinguished leaders of BJP and Former Deputy Prime Minister L.K. Advani in the first NDA Government led by BJP, had famously said with respect to secularism, that it is, "Justice for all, appeasement of none."

RSS does not crave Hindu domination as the layman in India has been led to believe. It is the hurt to Hindu sentiments that is being done to appease minorities over 70 years since India attained freedom, which is the point of concern. Most prominent among these concerns is the painful Ram Janmabhoomi issue—painful to the majority Hindu population of India, which has historically never interfered in any other community's religious activity or invaded anyone's country, and which yearns to see the restoration of Bhagwan Shri Ram Lalla's temple at the site where it was destroyed by Mughal invader Babur's hordes in the 16th century.

Amidst all this, it is a travesty that the largest opposition to RSS is from Hindus themselves, those Hindus who have been educated through Western-Christian models of schooling where the historic horrors and violence of the global advance of Christianity are never taught, but where Hindu students instead imbibe a culture of prejudice to their own origins, contempt to Vedic practices and Hindu cultural organizations. The RSS to them is seen as "communal" when no action of it ever would fit that description. Never has its outreach by volunteers in saving lives during disasters discriminated on caste and religion, and not one of RSS's affiliate organizations like schools, trade, farmer and student unions and others prevented any Indian from joining them. It is instructive to note that in Uttar Pradesh, for instance, the excellent schools run by Sewa Bharti, which have always had Muslim students, are now seeing an upsurge in Muslim student enrollment, according to news reports.

Relevant Then and Now

The RSS has followed the Hindu ethos of never publicizing Sewa and Daan. As a tradition, Hindus do not believe in letting anyone know about any act of kindness done by them because the belief is that it is one's duty to the society and motherland one belongs to. It is this Hindu belief that the RSS is inspired by. Neither is the prachaarak or swayamsevak supposed to feel any pride in what he does to help others. For 92 years, much of the Sewa that has been done all over India, in the remotest forests and deserts, in the mountains, plains and on the seashore, has gone unrecorded. Quite unlike Christian missionary organizations, for example, that publicise their work globally and seek donations on that basis. But the work of RSS swayamsevaks, who expect nothing in return, has quietly been impacting the lives of the people of India.

I can state with confidence that no other NGO but the RSS has continuously impacted Indian society across generations and still stays relevant. Generational Change is an aspect of the Sangh that not many know about. There is a continuous infusion of new leadership at all levels of the RSS and affiliate organizations. RSS is an aspirational organization. A Zilla Pracharak can be as young as 25 years and a Pracharak can be of any age. The direct administrative machinery of the RSS remains young.

It is heartening to see that with the advent of technology and social media, people across all ages and especially the young, are beginning to know more about the RSS. There is no official membership system but the RSS website shows a daily increase in online views and members. Today, the largely Left-oriented or pro-Congress Indian mainstream media in India is seeing a real challenge to its news domination and mind control of the people, a space it has owned for generations. Social media is seeing a robust exchange of information and the debunking of falsehoods about the RSS and its founder members that were propagated by mainstream media for decades.

An unbiased eye can see that far away from the disdainful urban elite class, it is the real people of India who are touched on a daily basis by the selfless sewa of the RSS workers. At the basic functional level of India, starting from the village—be it a personal family problem, a difference of opinion, a need for education or training, rescue during disaster, post-disaster rehabilitation and more, people turn to the RSS. This is an organization that lives in the people of India. Not only has the RSS not got its due so far, it has suffered continuous attacks on its ideology and functioning from the Indian media. This narrative is what is picked up by the Western media which then lends a communal character to a nationalistic organization that represents the cultural values of Hindus, who belong to a religion that has never expanded militarily or by force and violent conquest.

This book attempts to describe in a simple manner, the unparalleled work of the RSS since its inception, its history, the core of Sewa Karya, the structural organization, busting the myths of the RSS not having participated in the Independence movement of

India, the Ram Janmabhoomi issue, and the organisation's dynamic nature through Generational Change. I hope it will help enlighten you, the reader, about many aspects of the organization that you might not have known, and bring a sense of wonder at the service of the Sangh, whose swayamsevaks on the field touch millions of lives every day. Whose swayamsevaks died fighting for the freedom of India but we did not know. Swayamsevaks of the RSS, who work to keep the unity and confidence of India strong so that our ancient civilization continues to inspire the world as it has done for thousands of years.

BHARAT IS TRUSTEE FOR KNOWLEDGE THAT CAN BE CALLED AS GLOBAL DHARMA

"The image of Bharat is that we accept and welcome all diversities, it is the global Dharma that was nurtured here.

Bharat is trustee for all this knowledge and has given it to the world from time to time."

Sarsangchalak Shri Mohan Bhagwat ji,
September 2018 *RSS Lecture Series*

CHAPTER 1

Origin and History of RSS

"The Hindu culture is the life-breath of Hindustan. It is therefore clear that if Hindustan is to be protected, we should first nourish the Hindu culture. If the Hindu culture perishes in Hindustan itself, and if the Hindu society ceases to exist, it will hardly be appropriate to refer to the mere geographical entity that remains as Hindustan. Mere geographical lumps do not make a nation. The entire society should be in such a vigilant and organized condition that no one would dare to cast an evil eye on any of our points of honour.

Strength, it should be remembered, comes only through organization. It is therefore the duty of every Hindu to do his best to consolidate the Hindu society. The Sangh is just carrying out this supreme task. The present fate of the country cannot be changed unless lakhs of young men dedicate their entire lifetime for that cause. To mould the minds of our youth towards that end is the supreme aim of the Sangh."

Dr. Keshav Baliram Hedgewar, *Founder of RSS*

Most Indians take the Independence of India for granted, and the value of that hard won freedom is scarcely appreciated. This is especially because the post-Independence narrative in Indian history text books and popular news stories has focused more on certain freedom fighters who only spoke of freedom from the British. The great thinkers, philosophers and leaders who had the vision to think ahead—that for a country to survive and establish itself as a free nation, it also needs a strong cultural identity—have, by and large, been sidelined.

The fundamental question is—"Can there be a nation without Cultural Identity?" The clear answer is No. All over the world, nations define themselves by religion and language as unique cultural elements that constitute a cultural identity. For example, "Britain is a Christian country," is a statement that their Prime Ministers have clearly said in their public speeches. And this is despite the population of believing Protestant Christians being on a sharp decline in Britain—The 31st British Social Attitudes Survey, 2013, states that the percentage of people identifying as Church of England/Anglican has fallen from 27 per cent in 2003 to 16 per cent in 2013, a drop of a whopping 59 per cent.

The Indian identity was called Hindutva or Hindu view of life by such great minds as Dr Radhakrishnan and Shri Rabindranath Tagore. But it is only in India that the unfortunate inclusion of the word "secularism" in the Preamble to the Constitution by force of majority during then Prime Minister Indira Gandhi's draconian Emergency, has been taken so seriously that modern Indians have trained themselves into believing that the word secular stands for no religious or cultural identity!

Back in the early 20th century too, the majority of Indian National Congress (INC) leaders were westernized, educated elite, like Jawaharlal Nehru and M.A. Jinnah, who had not succeeded in making the call for Independence a mass movement of the people. It was after Gandhi ji returned to India from South Africa in 1915 and used cultural Hindu symbols and connection points like satyagraha, upvaas (fasting), *maun vrat* (vow of silence), that it resonated with the masses of India. Before that it was Shri Lokmanya Tilak who had energized the masses through Hindu cultural mobilizing activities in Maharashtra in 1893 like the Ganeshotsav and the powerful writings in his publication *Kesari.* As the Independence movement gained momentum after Gandhi ji's campaign, the separatist forces of Muslim leaders began to rear their heads and Gandhi ji's support to the Khilafat movement in Turkey and Indian Muslim support for the same in 1920 gave more strength to Muslim mobilization. What's more, Hindus too, persuaded by Gandhi ji, contributed to the Khilafat movement, without ever expecting the Muslim attacks on them that would come later! This action of Gandhi ji in supporting the Khilafat movement was not appreciated by many INC members who saw it as dangerous to the unity of the country.

The Moplah riots in Malabar in 1921 can be seen as a dangerous and very tragic impact of the support to militant Islamists during the Freedom Movement. Gandhi ji had persuaded Congress to support the Khilafat movement of the Muslims in India to insist on the British maintaining the authority of the Caliph of Islam—the Ottoman Sultan—after World War I, though the Turks had been defeated.

Leftist historians have painted the dastardly killings of Hindus by Muslims in the Malabar region of Kerala as an agrarian revolt but it was, in fact, a violent assertion of Islamic religious militancy on the back of the Khilafat movement. Muslims in Malabar went on a rampage attacking Hindus, killing, raping women and forcibly converting Hindus. Estimated deaths were close to 10,000 Hindus butchered and thousands of Hindus forcibly converted to Islam. Annie Besant, senior British leader of the Indian National Congress that had been started by A.O. Hume, reported how Hindus who would not convert to Islam were either killed or driven away. Dr B.R. Ambedkar in his writings referred to the Malabar incident as "brutal and unrestrained barbarism." But Dr Ambedkar noted that Gandhi ji, instead of criticizing the Moplahs for their inhuman violence, spoke of them as "brave God-fearing Moplahs who were fighting for what they consider as religion and in a manner which they consider as religious."

It was in these times that Dr Hedgewar, a staunch nationalist, and member of INC, began to feel dismay and shock as he saw the disastrous times that lay ahead for Hindus if they were not mobilized and united.

HINDU MAHASABHA AND VEER SAVARKAR – STIRRINGS OF HINDU NATIONALISM

Again a much vilified personality by Leftist historians, Shri Vinayak Damodar Savarkar (1883-1966), was undeniably one of the sharpest minds of his times. A lawyer, brilliant writer and politician, he got the title Veer after an incident where as a boy of 12 years, he mobilized Hindu boys to fight Muslims who had attacked them and defeated them though the Hindus were smaller in number. It was Veer Savarkar ji who created the term *Hindutva* that represented a unified identity of Hindus as the essence of India. Such was his advanced scholarly thinking that he tapped into the elements of existing theories like utilitarianism (optimum action is that which maximizes utility), rationalism (reason as source of knowledge), humanism, among others. Savarkar ji did not approve of orthodoxy and superstitious beliefs in any religion and was an atheist.

As a freedom fighter who believed in complete independence from the British by revolutionary means, Savarkar ji, while studying in England, was brave enough to start the Free India Society, an association of Indian students in Britain. His revolutionary activities eventually led to his arrest by the British in 1910. He was sentenced to two life terms of imprisonment totaling fifty years and was moved to the notoriously dangerous Andaman and Nicobar prison (Kala Pani). After suffering much torture and inhuman conditions, he was released in 1921.

It was in 1907 that Savarkar ji co-founded the Akhil Bharat Hindu Mahasabha along with other leaders like Pandit Madan Mohan Malviya and Lala Lajpat Rai. The organisation was intended to safeguard the rights of Hindus and defend the right to a Hindu Rashtra or a "National Home for the Hindu." The game changing book of Savarkar ji, "Hindutva," that he wrote when he was in jail, stated what it means to be a Hindu, and what Hindu pride and identity was about. All people descended from Hindu culture like Jains, Buddhist, and Sikhs were defined as being part of Hindutva.

After his release in 1921, he toured India extensively and was a powerful orator who kept his listeners spellbound with his articulation of Hindu political and social unity and a theme of Hindutva that had not been that well stated by anyone previously.

The threat to Hindu life and existence was serious in those times and we can see that it was thanks to leaders with foresight and courage like Veer Savarkar ji and Dr Hedgewar ji, that Hindus rights were protected in a chaotic period that saw India under foreign British control, the mobilization of Muslims at unprecedented levels and the Congress and Gandhi ji playing along to cater to extremist Muslim sentiments at the cost of Hindu rights and security and unity of India.

DR HEDGEWAR STARTS THE RSS

The articulation of an identity for Hindus by Veer Savarkar in *Hindutva* greatly inspired Dr Hedgewar ji, the founder of RSS and first Sarsangchalak, who was also inspired by the cultural nationalism of Lokmanya Bal Gangadhar Tilak ji. Dr Hedgewar or Doctor ji as he was fondly called, believed that Hindu religious and cultural heritage should be the foundational basis of Indian nationhood.

But how did a simple boy from Nagpur, Maharashtra—Keshav Baliram Hedgewar—born in 1889, grow into the powerful leader that he became later in life? Whose mission and vision lives on 93 years later?

He lost both parents when he was just thirteen years old to plague and his elder brothers took care of his education. Doctor ji showed his fighting spirit early on when he was thrown out of school in Nagpur for singing Vande Mataram which the British government had banned anyone from singing. Hence, he had to take up his further schooling in other towns.

It was Shri B.S. Moonje (National President of the Hindu Mahasabha) who persuaded Doctor ji after his matriculation in

1910 to pursue his medical studies in Kolkata. After this, he chose to come back to Nagpur and work as a doctor. He subsequently joined the Indian National Congress and was a strong nationalist who fought for Independence. But like several other Congress leaders of the time, the policies of Congress became a matter of concern to him and he became disheartened by the political movement.

The Moplah riots and other Muslim riots put Doctor ji into deep thought on the future of India as a united, strong nation, Hindu identity and the need for an alternate model of nation building that was rooted in India's Hindu religion and culture. He was very inspired by Chhatrapati Shivaji Maharaj, the first Hindu emperor who had successfully challenged the brutal Mughals who had bled the nation and tortured the people, and established a Hindu Maratha empire that under his successors and the Peshwas, spread to a large part of north, central and the Deccan region of India.

With no resources but just a burning fire of commitment in him, in 1925 on the sacred day of Vijaya Dashami, Dr Hedgewar founded the Sangh. With just 17 like-minded men with him, he said, "We are inaugurating Sangh today. All of us must train ourselves physically, intellectually and in every way so as to be capable of achieving our cherished goal." The goal was to organize Hindus on a cultural and spiritual basis to ensure India is free from foreign control. The formal start of Sangh took place in Doctor Hedgewar's humble home in 'Sukravari' in Nagpur. Training in drill, march etc. was imparted on Sundays. On Thursdays and Sundays there were discourses on national affairs.

The name 'Rashtriya Swayamsevak Sangh' was selected for Sangh on April 17, 1926, in a meeting called for this purpose at Dr. Hedgewar's house, from a list of four suggested names—Jaripatka Mandal, Bharat Uddharak Mandal, Hindu Swayamsevak Sangh, and Rashtriya Swayamsevak Sangh. Doctor ji's slogan was "Hinduism is Nationalism."

Subsequently, Nitya Shakhas (daily meetings), were started at Mohitewada ground in Nagpur. Lathi—'Danda'—was introduced in the Shakha. New commands such as Dakhsa, Aaram—were used for the first time in Shakhas. The tradition of commencing the daily activities with salutation to the Bhagwa Dhwaj and concluding with the prayer—Prarthana—in Hindi and Marathi was instituted.

The initial stage of Shakha expansion was in Maharashtra with only a little expansion in other states. Dr Hedgewar had once said that when one per cent of the people in villages and three per cent in the cities become Sangh swayamsevaks, RSS would be able to give a new turn to national life. With no resources and firm resolve, Dr Hedgewar was able to take RSS to further strength as a mission in just 15 years after its start. It was Doctorji's simple living and firm ideals that inspired the swayamsevaks. Doctor ji's humility is underlined by the fact that in 1933, addressing the swayamsevaks, he had said that he is not the founder of the Sangh, they are all the founding fathers of the Sangh and that he is only a cementing agent. He had said that he is willing to step down as Sarsangchalak if they wished to have another leader because for him a position or his own person as such was of no value and what is valuable is the mission they have all taken up.

EXPANSION OF THE SANGH UNDER GURUJI GOLWALKAR

The major expansion of the Sangh outside Maharashtra was under Pujaniya Guru ji Golwalkar. When he took over as Sarsangchalak in 1940 at a young 34 years, Shakhas outside Nagpur were estimated to be just around 30 in number. By 1945 Guruji had overseen the setting up of Shakhas in most major cities and towns of North India. Guru ji was an excellent organizer, spiritual teacher and a strong leader who ensured the rapid expansion of the Sangh.

Madhav Sadashiv Golwalkar ji was born near Nagpur In 1906 into a fairly prosperous family. Right from his school days he had a keen interest in spirituality. He was a good student and went on to study in a college run by Christian missionaries in Nagpur. It is said that it was in Hislop College where he saw Hinduism being vilified and Christianity advocated that he started to feel a sense of deep concern for Hinduism. He left the college and went on to complete his Bachelors and Masters degrees in Science from Benares Hindu University, Varanasi.

Pandit Madan Mohan Malaviya, a nationalist leader with strong Hindu cultural leanings and founder of BHU, was a great inspiration for Golwalkar ji. He went on to teach zoology in BHU for three years. Right since then, because he wore simple clothes, had a long beard, long hair, he was called 'Guruji' by his students (and this was how he was addressed even in the RSS). He was so loved by his students because he was a lecturer who truly cared for them, often going out of his way and spending money from his own salary to buy books for his students.

Interestingly, during his tenure as a lecturer, Golwalkar ji did not have any interest in the Shakhas of the Sangh. It was during that time that a BHU student who was also close to Doctor ji, Bhaiyaji Dani, started a shakha in Varanasi, the first one there. Golwalkar ji attended meetings and members regarded his views highly. But he did not seem to be too keen about the RSS. When Doctor ji visited Benares in 1931, he was intrigued by Golwalkar ji's Guru-like persona and his perspective.

When Guruji returned to Nagpur, he began to meet with Doctor ji more and it was Doctor ji who encouraged him to complete a law degree. Golwalkar ji obtained a law degree in 1935. Doctor ji made him *karyavah* of the main Nagpur shakha in 1934. After Guru ji began practising law, Doctor ji tasked him with the management of the Akola Officers' Training Camp.

But Guruji's life went on a different path when he felt he wanted to renounce the world and become a sanyasi. He gave up his law practice in 1936 and working for RSS to join the Ramakrishna Mission Ashram in Sargachi, West Bengal, as a disciple of Swami Akhandananda, who was a disciple of Sri Ramakrishna and a brother monk of Swami Vivekananda. Guru ji received his *dikhsha* to be ordained as a monk in 1937 but he left the Ashram quite soon as his Guru had passed away and he then returned to Nagpur. Guruji reportedly faced a low point in his life, confused and almost like in a state of depression. He approached Doctor ji for advice and that was when he convinced Guruji that his life would get a sense of purpose by fulfilling his duties to society which could be best achieved through working for the Sangh.

Doctor ji's sharp instincts sensed the unique commitment and capability of Guruji as a leader. Guru ji had excellent competency as an organizer—he could manage a large camp with various sub-divisions, was a powerful and inspiring orator, very well-read and a very good writer. He was, in a sense, being groomed for a larger leadership role. Guruji was appointed Sarkaryavah of the RSS in 1939.

It was during a very serious illness of Doctor ji that he realized that the Sangh needed a new leader and a day before he died in June 1940, in front of the Swayamsevaks present, Doctor ji handed over the charge of Sarsangchalak to Guru ji. Guru ji himself was a little unsure because he was still quite new in the Sangh and did not have a national profile as such. It was still early days for the RSS and many supporters too were unsure about whether the RSS would survive after Doctor ji's passing.

But not just survive, under Guruji's leadership, the RSS grew to tremendous heights. Under Guruji as Sarsangchalak for over 30 years, RSS became one of the strongest cultural organisations in India. Its membership expanded manifold from 100,000 when he took over to 10,00,000 in those decades. Guruji oversaw the setting up of 50 affiliate organizations, thereby giving RSS a representation in all major fields of activity—educational, farming, labour, tribal welfare, social service, student outreach. The organisation's footprint expanded to foreign shores too with the setting up of Hindu Swayamsevak Sangh in Kenya and then in other countries.

But Guruji's work was not easy. Amidst murmurs of discontent when he took over in 1940, Guruji gave his first speech to the swayamsevaks, as Sarsangchalak. He said, "Doctorji was a synthesis of an affectionate mother, a responsible father and an able Guru. He has entrusted me with this tough job of Sarsanghachalak, but then this is the throne of Vikramaditya (a king of ancient India known for his benevolence and justice); even if a shepherd boy would sit on it, he would but dispense justice.... The meritorious deeds of our great leader would ensure that I will always do the rightful things." Subsequently, in another speech, he said, "Our organization is like an impregnable fort; those who would attack it would only receive its brunt." The Swayamsevaks saw a strong leader in Guruji and knew the RSS was safe under him.

After Independence, the RSS saw that there was a dire need to reshape the entire educational system that had been influenced heavily by Lord Macaulay's game plan to erase all Indian cultural knowledge and pride in the same among Indians by creating an English educated Indian elite who would follow the philosophy of their White masters. In *A Bunch of Thoughts* (1966), Guruji wrote what he had observed after Independence, "Thus, after the quitting of the British, we find ourselves in a confused state of affairs trying to catch at something of each of the foreign theories and 'isms'. This is highly humiliating to a country, which has given rise to an all-comprehensive philosophy, capable of furnishing the true and abiding basis for construction of national life on political, economic, social and all other planes. It would be sheer bankruptcy of our intellect and originality if we believe that human intelligence has reached its zenith with the present theories and 'isms' of the West. Let us therefore evolve our own way of life based on the eternal truths discovered by our ancient seers and tested on the touchstone of reason, experience and history."

In 1952, the first "Saraswati Shishu Mandir" (nursery school) was founded in Gorakhpur, Uttar Pradesh, as an attempt towards inculcating, along with mandatory academic knowledge, discipline, patriotic outlook, love for one's own language, high moral values and Hindu principles the thrust of education being based upon a holistic approach to the physical, intellectual, moral and spiritual growth of the pupil. More focus on education continued subsequently as well as outreach to tribals and vanvasis through Bharatiya Vanvasi Kalyan Ashram (1952) and Bharatiya Mazdoor Sangh (1955).

UNDER TRYING TIMES GURUJI AND RSS STAND STRONG

After Independence, the country saw its most difficult times and Guruji led the RSS through Independence and Partition of India, his own unfair arrests (two times imprisoned) and the first ban on the RSS, several wars, huge natural disasters and the Goa Liberation Movement.

RSS was greatly pained during the tragic Partition of India, leading to the largest ever mass migration in human history and the deaths of 6 million people. The RSS swayamsevaks supported the Hindus and Sikhs who fled in fear from the newly formed nation for Muslims, Pakistan. With the advance of Communism in the 1940s as a challenger to the Congress and inner disagreements among RSS members, Guruji had to take on many challenges. While the older members wanted RSS to continue with its cultural work, the younger members asked for a stronger, activist model of the organization to support Hindus. Guruji was able to balance these different strands and lead the RSS to increase its national presence and incorporated a reverence for nature in the organization.

Socialism, Economy and RSS: Guruji was not only able to steer the organisation with his strong leadership and spiritual aura, he took strategic decisions to pivot the ideology as beyond the advancement of Hinduism and as one that is anti-Communism and Socialism. Such was his foresight that Guruji *saw in the 1940s, the dangers of this divisive foreign movement of Communism* that, as we have seen in history, was later responsible for the largest mass slaughter of humans, and the destruction of economies worldwide. He coined the slogan, "Not Socialism, but Hinduism." This was unique for its times as Communist ideology had taken over large parts of the world and had influenced the minds of many intellectuals and political leaders.

One among such Socialists was Pandit Jawaharlal Nehru who, after becoming Prime Minister of India in 1947, gave such a strong socialist slant to the economy that India lost out on the advantages that it had earned under the British with successful Indian business and industry; economic data shows how India's economy slumped in the decades after Independence with excessive state control. At Independence, India was estimated to have an economy of Rs 162 lakh crore in today's Rupee value terms, which most nations in Asia could not boast of at the time. To offer a perspective, if we consider the colossal destruction of Japan after World War II in 1945 where most of its physical economy was ruined, India was in a much better shape at its Independence. But Japan rebuilt itself by the force of national will and strong leadership, not socialism. Between 1947 and 1964, Compounded Annual Growth Rate (CAGR) for Japan's GDP per capita was a phenomenal 7.9 per cent, for the USSR 4.4 per cent and for India 1.68 per cent. Just looking at these figures tells us what happened to the Indian economy after Independence under Congress. Businessmen were treated as pariahs by Nehru. Hence, this clear, fair and sensible stand of the RSS under Guruji as being anti-Marxist, was appreciated by businessmen.

Swayamsevaks led the charge in Sewa after 1950, that Guruji had told all to focus on, be it relief work after the devastating Assam earthquake of 1950, and during the Indo-China War of 1962, wars with Pakistan in 1965 and 1971. Further, as the Goa, Dadra and Nagar Haveli region was still not free after 1947 as it was under the Portugese, swayamsevaks, risking their own lives, played a lead role in the Goa Liberation Movement.

Guruji saw through some of the most difficult times for the Sangh including the ban on it after the assassination of Gandhi ji (more in this chapter in a later section) and his unfair arrest along with the arrest of thousands of swayamsevaks. But his firm resolve was successful in the end. In fact, after 1948, the need for the Sangh in India was being debated on outside of the organisation, since a nation for Muslims, Pakistan, had already taken form and hence it was felt there would be no strife between Hindus and Muslims. But Guruji's guidance was firm in that the Sangh was not started to conflict with anyone and nor was it for countering any attack. "The main objective of the Sangh is character-building of the nation.... If the Hazrat Mohammed Saheb had not been born and Hindu society had been disoriented as at present, the organization of Hindus by the Sangh would have been as inevitable as it is today," he had said.

It is instructive to note that unlike others in India who conveniently pin the blame of their own shortcomings on others, Guruji was not one among them. He did not blame external agencies for the problems of Hindu society but spoke of the need to strengthen the society.

The Congress Party was clearly threatened by the rise of the Sangh and its close connect with Indians, and so decided without any basis to arrest Guruji on 1 February 1948, after Gandhi ji's assassination on 30 January 1948, and ban the Sangh for promoting "violence and subversion," as the government chose to call it (this was despite the fact that the assassin Shri Nathuram Godse had said he acted on his will). RSS swayamsevaks grew restive and Guru ji's huge base of supporters all over the country was angry at this unfair arrest. Guru ji appealed to them to re-start the Shakhas. *This movement, started on 9 December 1948, was called Satyagraha.*

Congress initially mocked at this Satyagraha but its party members were stunned to see that this Satyagraha had 77,090 Swayamsevaks as supporters who were jailed in different prisons. Indians saw an unmatched non-violent Satyagraha by the Swayamsevaks, who did not react despite terrible cruelty meted out on them by the police. Congress realized that Guruji was no small leader, because no Satyagraha by INC had ever seen nearly 80,000 participants. Eventually, the Sangh was cleared of any involvement in Gandhi ji's assassination after an enquiry. The ban was revoked in July 1949 when, as required by the government, the RSS drafted and submitted a written Constitution that was accepted by the Deputy Prime Minister and Home Minister Sardar Patel.

We must not forget here that Mahatma Gandhi had desired that the INC should be disbanded after India attained Independence as that was the INC's main objective. Only with INC disbanded could political parties representing the people in a democracy take off after Independence, but as we know, that did not happen, as the INC members only cared for power, and held a vice-like grip on the nation at the Centre for over 60 years even though many states formed their own parties and routed the Congress during this time. With no firm ideology, we can see how over the decades the INC split several times demonstrating its lack of commitment to a larger cause and this is still the case. Though RSS cannot be compared to the INC as RSS is not a political organization, the RSS has stood strong and expanded in leaps and bounds over the decades despite severe opposition and bans on it.

GURUJI WANTED THE CONSTITUTION OF INDIA TO REFLECT INDIA'S UNIQUE CULTURAL ETHOS

It is interesting that in today's times, we see a clash between cultural norms and laws framed by the Constitution of India that do not take our unique, ancient cultural practices into account. We have seen this in the raging issue of Sabarimala Temple in Kerala from September 2018. Kerala is the most educated state in India and highly educated believing Hindu women too have objected to what they call the Supreme Court's interference in allowing all women of reproductive age into the sacred ancient shrine of Swami Ayyappa who is a naistika brahmachari (eternal celibate). Which then implies that it is not lack of education that defines any imported concept of "opposition to patriarchy" (many of the believing Hindu women are from matriarchal families themselves) but that personal religious beliefs followed by Hindus in India differ from place to place and are entirely the preserve of those communities. This matter is being hotly debated on social media and mainstream media as well as by Indians in all forums on whether our Constitution really represents the people.

Going back in time, after the Constituent Assembly adopted the Constitution of India on 26 November 1949, an editorial was put out in the RSS magazine, Organiser, that, in keeping with the principle of freedom of speech, put forth Guruji's opinion. His opinion strikes a chord even today:

> *"Our Constitution too is just a cumbersome and heterogeneous piecing together of various articles from various Constitutions of Western countries. It has absolutely nothing, which can be called our own. Is there a single word of reference in its guiding principles as to what our national mission is and what our keynote in life is? No!"*

Guruji realized his own failing health and in 1973 selected Shri Balasaheb Deoras as the next Sarsangchalak. Once Guruji was asked, "Who after you?" and he promptly replied, "Why not you?" By that he meant that the Sangh was not working because of him alone.

Guruji's last message in 1973, was a powerful one and underlined the importance of the organization being bigger than individuals and that just like how a split happened in Congress, people expect that to happen to RSS too. But that will not happen because the members settle differences of opinion with goodwill and understanding as the organization is bigger than individuals.

Today, we in India see organized, violent and divisive movements on a regular basis, citing bogus claims of discrimination which are organized by vested interests with tacit foreign support that's being reported in the media as well. All this, only because they are enraged that a strong, nationalist government led by the BJP is in power at the Centre.

An extract from that last message of Guruji is a powerful reminder for all Indians today:

"... Today, disintegrating forces are afoot in our country and the foreign powers are lying in wait to fish in the troubled waters. Some years back, the foreign powers had their hand behind the language conflict in Assam. Now it seems there is the foreign hand in the circulation of exaggerated news of persecution of Harijans. The foreign powers know very well that they can retain their supremacy in this country only by splitting the Hindus.

We must admit that we have not been successful, to the extent expected of us, in integrating the society and rousing the feeling of intense patriotism in it. As such, we have to be more keenly conscious of our responsibility, think about all aspects of our work, and put ourselves to the wheel wholeheartedly and with a resolve to reach the goal at all costs in the near future. Representatives from various parts of the country have assembled here, and I am sure they will assuredly put in all possible efforts in their respective spheres in this direction.

Today I have spoken—who knows whether God will allow me another opportunity!"

Guruji Golwalkar's last message

DEORAS JI—A TALL LEADER DURING THE EMERGENCY AND AFTER

When Madhukar Dattatreya Deoras ji, also called Balasaheb Deoras ji, took charge as Sarsangchalak in 1973 (until 1993 when he relinquished office due to ill health), he was about to lead the RSS through another very epochal and stressful period in India's history as well as that of the RSS—the Emergency (1975-77) imposed by then Prime Minister Indira Gandhi, the rise of the Bharatiya Jan Sangh and the subsequent phenomenal growth of the BJP seeing it in power at the Cebtre (Deoras ji was alive when Shri Atal Behari Vajpayee ji became Prime Minister in 1996).

Deoras ji said after taking over as Sarsangchalak, "I do not have a natural talent like Dr Hedgewar, nor do I have a towering personality like Sri Guruji. Whatever heights the Sangh work has reached, it is because of these two great personalities. I can do justice to this responsibility only on the basis of rare set of karyakartas with Sangh."

"THE NATION AND STATE ARE DIFFERENT CONCEPTS": BHAURAO DEORAS

Shri Bhaurao Deoras ji, RSS Pracharak and brother of Shri Balasaheb Deoras ji, had said in an interview in 1990 that Nation and State are two different concepts.

"States have equal rights, equal citizenship—that is the concept of state. This nation is not created by the British or anything. It is there from a long time, from

Ram, from Krishna—thousands of years ago. The whole country had that concept of Ram, the concept of Krishna, the concept of Mahabharata, etc. Anywhere you go you will find the same thing. That is the binding thing. Culture was the binding factor throughout the country. There may be different kings, different rulers in the last 1,000 years or something like that ... then the foreigners came and all that."

Impetus to Sewa: It was under Deoras ji that Sewa or service got a huge impetus so that the most underprivileged communities could get access to essential education, healthcare and livelihood. Such was his commitment that he visited hundreds of villages and project sites to personally oversee the works. A little after he took over as Sarsangchalak, he said in a speech in Pune (1974): *"If untouchability is not wrong, nothing is wrong."* Deoras ji realized the need for equality and bringing all people together with no discrimination on caste lines. He was a strong advocate of reservations for Dalits and Scheduled Caste persons.

In the 1970s Prime Minister Smt Indira Gandhi was disturbed by the growing people's movements and students protests nation-wide against corruption and rampant misrule under Congress. The Jayprakash Narayan movement had taken the nation by storm and students had risen in revolt against a dictatorial government. It was to ensure that her power remained without question, that for no reason that can be justified by evidence, Smt Indira Gandhi imposed the National Emergency all of a sudden on the night of June 25, 1975. This put the nation into a tizzy and the suspension of Fundamental Rights including Right to Freedom of Speech and Expression (with severe censorship of media) and Assembly, among others, cracked down on the voice of rightful protest in a democracy. It was the murder of democracy during the Emergency. Over 1,40,000 people were arrested without trial, over 8 million forced sterilizations (a number that beat even those in Nazi Germany) were organized during the Emergency leading to many deaths, and many other incidents of brutality.

Deoras' ji saw the most difficult period during the Emergency as the RSS was banned and he, along with 30,000 others, were held under the draconian Maintenance of Internal Security Act. Under the Defence of India Rules, another 75,000 were detained. This included Shri Jayprakash Narayan, Shri Morarji Desai ji, Maharani Vijayraje Scindia, Maharani Gayatri Devi as well as those who would emerge later as the tallest leaders in BJP, like Shri Vajpayee ji and Shri Advani ji, The nation-wide gloom and fear and the situation among RSS swayamsevaks can well be imagined. But Deoras ji not only motivated the swayamsevaks but also guided the largest non-violent satyagraha movement in Independent India, in secret.

RSS swayamsevaks formed underground movements for the restoration of democracy. They enabled those writings that had been censored in the media to be published and distributed on a large scale through their underground network. Networks were established between leaders of different political parties who had been jailed and those outside jail to co-ordinate this brave movement. International magazine The Economist in its December 1976 issue described the movement as *"the only non-Left revolutionary force in the world."* It noted that the movement was "dominated by tens of thousands of RSS cadres, though more and more young recruits are coming."

Smt Indira Gandhi was known for her political cunning and knew that RSS was a very strong organization. After the Emergency was called off in 1977, when she finally announced the elections on January 23 1977, she knew that if RSS did not support the opposition Janata Party, they could not win against her. She thus spoke with Deoras ji and said she would revoke the RSS ban if it did not support the Janata Party.

Deoras ji of course, firmly declined her offer. The Janata Party, in alliance with the Bharatiya Jan Sangh and other parties, formed the first non-Congress Government of independent India with Shri Morarji Desai ji as Prime Minister (1977-1979). Though it did not complete its full term, it marked a sea change in political and public perception in that there are alternatives to the Congress party. After the disagreement of Bharatiya Jan Sangh with the Janata Party, it also led to the formation of the Bharatiya Janata Party (BJP) from the original Jan Sangh. And this marked a totally new turn in the decades to come in Indian politics and governance.

Indira Gandhi was back in power in January 1980 and with her increasing backing of Sikh religious extremists to strengthen her Sikh vote base, there were signs of imminent danger. Deoras ji worked hard to prevent divisions between Hindus and Sikhs. One Pracharak from each state was sent to Punjab and worked tirelessly on the ground to ensure unity between Hindus and Sikhs despite several RSS workers being killed and even a direct attack on a RSS shakha.

In Assam too, Deoras ji ensured swayamsevaks spread the cause of grievances of Assam agitators to all parts of India, and also held meetings and distributed writings on the dangers on illegal infiltration from Bangladesh. The infamous conversions of Dalits to Islam by monetary inducements in Meenakshipuram in Tirunelveli, Tamil Nadu, created huge outrage nation-wide; this was also addressed by Swayamsevaks. Deoras ji said that greater unity is necessary among Hindus to prevent such conversions. Vishwa Hindu Parishad launched the historic "Ekatmata Yatra" wherein three yatras, two from north to south and one from east to west, along with thousands of small yatras across the country, touched 1.5 lakh villages went through almost all the districts in India. Many of those who converted in Meenakshipuram came back to the Hindu fold. Deoras ji oversaw the RSS playing a key role in the Ram Janmabhoomi agitation for a Shri Ram Mandir in Ayodhya.

Shri Deoras ji was recognized for his excellent consensus building ability as seen with Janata Party and others and was seen as a great team player. He was also not one to shy away from risk taking as can be seen from all that he led the RSS through during his tenure. Deoras ji gave Shri Atal Behari Vajpayee ji complete freedom to construct the BJP on the principle of "Gandhian socialism."After the party performed poorly in 1984 general elections, it was Deoras ji who as Sarsangchalak, mended bridges between RSS and BJP, and brought in more swayamsevaks into the BJP to help it further. More than political power, Deoras ji had a vision of a united India with Hindu consolidation, and no discrimination or divisions on caste or creed.

Deoras ji was a diabetic even when he had taken charge of the RSS in 1973 but became the first RSS chief to relinquish the post in 1993 and hand over charge to Shri Rajendra Singh ji, when he realised his health was failing. Shri Rajendra ji had been an active freedom fighter during the Quit India Movement and though he was Sarsangchalak for only six years, this was a very critical period in India's political history and marked the entry of the BJP as ruling party at the Centre for the first time in 1996, even if it was for only 13 days. Later in 1998 the National Democratic Alliance government was formed with BJP as the lead party and Vajpayee ji as Prime Minister. Under Rajendra ji, BJP's seat share increased to 182 and NDA formed the government again in 1999. Rajendra ji was known to have had excellent relations with political leaders across the spectrum and intellectuals.

Due to his health problems, he gave up the position of Sarsangchalak in February 2000 and nominated Shri K.S. Sudarshan ji to take over. Due to health issues Shri Sudarshan ji stepped down from the position of Sarsangchalak and Dr Mohan Bhagwat took over as Sarsangchalak in March 2009.

RSS Banned Once by British, Thrice Since Independence

Right since its inception, RSS has been looked at as a threat by the British—and that is quite understandable, as they feared the revolt of the masses of Indians against them and knew the RSS was a unifying, nationalist force. It is instructive to note that while the British as colonisers, did sometimes try to put restrictions on the RSS on communicating literature and having shakha meetings, it banned the RSS only once and for four days! Whereas the RSS was banned three times in independent India!

The ban by the British on the RSS was in the Punjab Province of British India on January 24, 1947, and the Muslim National Guard was also banned then. This ban on RSS was revoked four days later on January 28, 1947. The greatest irony is that the history of repression of a nationalist organization like the RSS is far worse after India gained Independence; all bans on the organization were by Congress governments! This shows how the Congress party feared the RSS even more than the British did and was wary of any organization that could threaten its controlling position in India or question it when required.

(i) Ban on RSS after Gandhi ji's Assassination (1948)

The period of Independence and the months after were a traumatic period for Indians—freedom brought with it the pain of our Motherland being divided on the demand of Muslims for a separate nation, Pakistan.

Mahatma Gandhi was assassinated on the morning of January 30, 1948, in Birla House, by Shri Nathuram Vinayak Godse. The people of India were shocked and saddened by the assassination of Gandhi ji. RSS Sarsangchalak Guruji Golwalkar was in Madras (now Chennai) at a meeting when he heard the news and was deeply pained by the killing of Mahatma Gandhi. He was just about to take a sip of tea, when this news was passed on to him and he put his cup down and said, "What a misfortune for the country." Immediately, he sent condolence telegrams to PM Nehru, Union Home Minister Sardar Patel and Shri Devdas Gandhi, the fourth and youngest son of Mahatma Gandhi. Guruji cancelled all his appointments for an all India tour and rushed back to Nagpur.

For all the lies spread about RSS having celebrated Gandhi ji's assassination, it is important to note that *Guruji ordered all shakhas to be closed for 13 days in mourning,* such was the depth of respect that

RSS had towards Gandhi ji. This was the first time ever that the shakhas were ordered to be closed as never has there been a break in shakha activity since RSS was founded in 1925.

In his letter to Sardar Patel, Guruji wrote: "Let us shoulder the responsibility that has fallen upon us by the untimely passing away of that great unifier, keeping alive the sacred memories of that soul who had tied diverse natures in a single bond and was leading them all on a single path. And let us, with the right feelings, restrained tone and fraternal love, conserve our strength and cement the national life with everlasting oneness."

But in a shocking reaction from the government, Guruji was arrested on 1 February 1948 and RSS was banned on February 4 that year. This action was taken merely on the basis that Godse had many years ago been a member of RSS but that he had left RSS in 1940 was not taken into consideration. Shockingly, Guruji was arrested under the notorious Bengal State Prisoners Act, an Act which Nehru had himself condemned before Independence and called a 'black law!' The law empowered the administration to detain an individual indefinitely, on the basis of suspicion of criminal intent, and without having to commit the detenu to trial.

Guruji was released six months later in August 1948, and he wrote to PM Nehru to lift the ban on the RSS. Nehru replied that the matter was under the Home Minister (Sardar Patel) and Golwalkar approached him. Sardar Patel then placed a condition that the RSS adopt a formal written Constitution and make it public, and several other preconditions. Patel even asked Guruji to have RSS join the Congress but Guruji refused. He was arrested again.

Swayamsevaks of RSS organized a peaceful satyagraha and over 77,000 voluntarily got arrested. In fact, it was the energetic students and youth, which until then were active only in Shakhas, who were mobilised to contact the public with issues of national interest, particularly the draft Constitution of India which was then being debated in the Constituent Assembly. (This movement, the Akhil

Bharatiya Vidyarthi Parishad (ABVP), in the course of time, grew into a massive nation-wide student organisation, successfully channelizing the energy, talent and creativity in students, taking time out after completing educational responsibilities, for nation-building activities. ABVP is today the leading student organisation in India with a nationalist ethos and growing membership.)

The Congress was naturally taken aback by the masses that supported RSS. Meanwhile, investigations that were going on since Gandhi ji's assassination reported that there was no link between RSS and the perpetrator Godse's action. *The government could not find any evidence against the RSS.* RSS drafted a Constitution and on 11 July 1949, the ban on the RSS was lifted.

PREAMBLE TO CONSTITUTION OF THE RASHTRIYA SWAYAMSEVAK SANGH (1949)

"Whereas in the disintegrated conditions of the country it was considered necessary to have an Organisation:

(a) *To eradicate the fissiparous tendencies arising from diversities of sect, faith, caste and creed and from political, economic, linguistic and provincial differences, amongst Hindus;*
(b) *To make them realise the greatness of their past;*
(c) *To inculcate in them a spirit of service, sacrifice and selfless devotion to the Hindu Samraj, as a whole;*
(d) *To build up an organised and well disciplined corporate life; and*
(e) *To bring about an all-round regeneration of Hindu Samaj.]*

Policy - Article 4:

(a) The Sangh believes in orderly evaluation of the Society and adheres to peaceful and legitimate means for the realisation of its ideals.
(b) In consonance with the cultural heritage of the Hindu Samraj, the Sangh has abiding faith in the fundamental principle of tolerance towards all faiths. The Sangh as such, has no politics and is devoted to purely cultural work. The individual Swayamsevaks, however, may join any political party, except such parties as believe in or resort to violent and secret methods to achieve their ends; persons owing allegiance to such parties or believing in such methods shall have no place in the Sangh."

Interestingly, under Indira Gandhi's government, a judicial commission under Justice JL Kapur, a retired Supreme Court judge, was set up. After the examination of 101 witnesses and 407 documents, the Kapur Commission's report was published in 1969. It clearly stated that the evidence shows that RSS did not have a hand in Mahatma Gandhi's murder, that Godse was not a member of the RSS and that there was no evidence that RSS was indulging in violent activities against Gandhi ji or top Congress leaders.

During these times, it must be mentioned that *The Goa Liberation Movement* was one that grew strong due to the involvement of swayamsevaks. It started in the 19th century to demand freedom of Goa, Dadra and Nagar Haveli from the Portugese, it was in the period of 1940-'61 that it gained momentum. The Portugese were brutal colonizers and had invaded Goa 500 years earlier. Forced conversions of Hindu populations to Christianity at the point of death were being carried out and the local population was angry.

In 1954, young men from Azad Gomatak Dal in which there were many swayamsevaks, launched an attack on Dadra and Nagar Haveli and captured it from the Portugese. Many swayamsevaks lost their lives. RSS leaders demanded that the Indian government end Portuguese rule in Goa by armed attack. PM Nehru refused to do so and RSS leader Shri Jagannath Rao Joshi ji led a satyagraha with thousands of men on 23 June 1955. Joshi ji and his supporters were imprisoned by the Portuguese police force. Satyagraha continued but was met with brute force. On 15 August 1955, Portuguese police fired at unarmed satyagrahis, killing 20 or so people, many of whom were swayamsevaks. Diplomatic efforts with the Portugese had failed and realizing that force would be needed to free Goa, Nehru ordered the Indian Armed Forces to capture Goa. A military operation was conducted 18-19 December 1961, and Indian troops captured Goa. The Governor-General of Portuguese India signed an instrument of surrender.

Again, it was the RSS that selflessly helped soldiers during the ***1962 Indo-China*** War after China attacked India and some even volunteered to fight along with the Indian Army and got killed in the war. Unofficial records estimate 43 swayamsevaks died fighting in this war. This forced even the RSS' worst critics in Congress to acknowledge the swayamsevaks' contribution.

This clearly demonstrated that the RSS held no ill will to the Government of India because for the RSS it was India that was above all. Such was Guruji's generosity that when everyone criticized Nehru for the China war (a legitimate criticism), he, however, said that in that hour of crisis, instead of criticizing, everyone should stand with the government. Guruji even stopped a series of articles in the RSS magazine *Organiser* that had attacked Nehru's blunders with regard to China.

The immense contribution of RSS resulted in Nehru amending his opinion of the Sangh. RSS was invited to participate in the Republic Day parade of 1963 along with swayamsewaks in full uniform.

(ii) Ban on RSS during the Emergency (1975-77)

Indira Gandhi imposed the National Emergency all of a sudden on the night of 25 June 1975. With the suspension of Fundamental Rights including Right to Freedom of Speech and Expression and severe censorship of media, democracy was strangled. Over 1,40,000 people were arrested without trial, over 8 million forced sterilizations (a number that beat those done in Nazi Germany) were organized during the Emergency leading to many deaths, and many other incidents of brutality.

The RSS saw its second ban since Independence during the Emergency and Sarsangchalak Deoras ji, along with 30,000 others, were held under the Maintenance of Internal Security Act. Also arrested were swayamsevaks and Bharatiya Jan Sangh leaders like Vajpayee ji, Advani ji and Arun Jaitley ji, Strong movements led by Jayaprakash Narayan and others were taking certain states in North India by storm like in Bihar. Deoras ji even wrote letters to PM Smt Indira Gandhi and assured her of RSS's co-operation in return for the revoking the ban, saying that RSS had no connection with these movements in other states. When all negotiations proved futile, Deoras ji motivated swayamsevaks and led the largest non-violent satyagraha movement in Independent India, in secret. The ban on the RSS was lifted after the Emergency was called off in 1977.

It is pertinent to note that despite the brutal suppression of the activities of swayamsevaks, the RSS grew in strength and in a way, saw that a vision of nationalism was necessary in the political space too.

- The Communist Party of India (CPI) supported the Emergency and so was not banned.
- Jamaat-e-Islami Hind (JIH), an offshoot of Jamaat-e-Islami that was founded in 1941, was banned during Emergency but not once before that.
- The notorious and now banned Students Islamic Movement of India (SIMI) that was founded in Aligarh in 1977, was banned only after the horrific terror attacks of 9/11 in the US. The three bans on it have been only after terror incidents happened.

(iii) Ban after Fall of Babri Masjid (1992)

It is important to note that the RSS was not at the forefront of the Ram Mandir Movement in the past. This movement was being led by the Vishwa Hindu Parishad and the Ram Janmabhoomi Nyas, an organization of Hindu saints promoted by VHP. It was in the mid-1980s, when in a meeting with leaders of the organisation from all the states, the then RSS Sarsangchalak Shri Balasaheb Deoras ji had asked: "Should the RSS plunge fully into the Ram Janmabhoomi movement or allow it to be led by the Vishwa Hindu Parishad and the Ram Janmabhoomi Nyas?" The assembled leaders from all over the country unanimously supported the idea of the RSS getting into the movement. The BJP adopted a resolution on the Ram Janmabhoomi issue at the meeting of its National Executive in Palampur, Himachal Pradesh, in June 1989. In this resolution, the BJP endorsed the demand for handing over Shri Ram Janmabhoomi to Hindus for the construction of a Ram Temple. But nowhere has

RSS ever asked for any structure to be destroyed. The outpouring of pain on 6 December 1992, by kar sevaks was a spontaneous reaction.

But still the organization was banned by the government of Prime Minister PV Narasimha Rao. In its July 1999 report, the Unlawful Activities Prevention Tribunal appointed by the Central Government headed by Justice P. K. Bahri, said that in its report submitted in 1993, they had not found anything unlawful in the activities of the RSS. Justice Bahri had upheld the ban imposed on the VHP (ban on VHP was lifted in 1995) by the Government but not on the RSS and the Bajrang Dal; the ban on the RSS and Bajrang Dal was lifted. A White Paper of Government of India dismissed the idea that the demolition was pre-organised.

CHAPTER 2

Unique Structural Organisation

It is the unique structural organisation of RSS that enables this seamless integration of the Sangh network with the needs of the society it serves. The RSS does not have any formal membership process. Men and boys can become members by joining the nearest shakha, the basic unit of functioning. Though there are no official membership records, RSS is estimated to have over 90 lakh members.

Interestingly, if one meets any swayamsevak, he will say "I am an ordinary swayamsevak," when some of the work he would have done would have been extraordinary such as saving lives risking his own, bringing education to tribals in remote forests and the like. But such is the humility of the RSS that nowhere does ego enter a swayamsevak's conscience.

It is the swayamsevak who is at the core of the organization. There is an old anecdote about Dr Hedgewar, the founder of RSS, who had once appealed to his swayamsevak brothers to have someone else take over the responsibility of Sarsangchalak (chief) so that he could work as an ordinary swayamsevak. Though the situation was such that he was unable to do so, this underlines the amount of pride that a person has in being a swayamsevak in the RSS.

In the words of Sarsangchalak Shri Bhagwat ji: "Sangh means all the swayamsevaks together and all the swayamsevaks form the Sangh,"

NO FORMAL MEMBERSHIP, SHAKHA AS FUNDAMENTAL UNIT

The *Shakha* is the fundamental unit of activity of RSS and since there is no formal membership (no fees, registration form, and formal application) any Indian can approach the nearest Shakha and become a swayamsevak. The daily shakha meets twice a day and once the person starts attending the daily *shakha* either in the morning or evening as per their convenience, they become the *swayamsevak* of RSS.

As of March 2018, there are 58,967 daily *shakhas* being held at 37,190 places (including rural and urban), in addition to weekly gatherings at 16,405 places and monthly meetings at 7,976 locations in India.

Shakha is a daily gathering of Sangh Swayamsevaks of different age groups at a predefined meeting place or ground for one hour. Daily routine programmes include physical exercises, singing patriotic songs, group discussions on many themes and a prayer for our motherland.

But a *shakha* is not just that. It was the third Sarsanghchalak of RSS, the late Sri Balasaheb Deoras, who played a fundamental role in putting Sewa at the core of RSS and thus the *shakha*, as a means to develop the physical and emotional personality of the individual, to enable him to become capable of true service. He had called the *Shakha* a University for training *swayamsevaks*. Sri Deoras had once said:

"The RSS Shakha is not just a place to play games or parade, but an unsaid promise of the protection of the good citizenry, an acculturation forum to keep the young away from undesirable addictions; it is a centre of hope, for rapid action and undemanding help in case of emergencies and crisis that affect the people. It is a guarantee of the unafraid movement of women and a powerful deterrent to the indecent behaviour towards them, also a powerful threat to the brutal and anti-national forces. But the most important aspect is it is a university for training the appropriate workers to be made available for the requirements of the various fields of life of the nation. And the medium to achieve all this is the games we play on the grounds of RSS *Shakha*."

As members start attending *shakha* they participate in physical exercises and parade that is the integral part of RSS training. They are introduced to physical and psychological discipline. Doing physical exercises together helps in developing a sense of unity among the *swayamsevaks* hailing from different socio-economic and educational backgrounds. A definite uniform is a part of this discipline and is used only for certain ceremonial parades and functions.

It can be said that the daily Shakha, conceived of by Dr Hedgewar ji with his exemplary vision, is the most visible symbol of the RSS. Laypersons are often amazed that after 92 years since the inception of the Sangh, a simple tool like the daily Shakha can produce nationalists of such merit. The *Shakha* can be seen as the training ground for several of India's tallest leaders like Guruji Golwalkar and Pandit Deendayal Upadhyaya, and has given India such staunchly nationalist leaders such as former Prime Minister Late Atal Behari Vajpayee, L.K. Advani, and the current Indian Prime Minister Narendra Modi.

The Shakha has a saffron flag (called the *Bhagwa Dhwaj*) in the middle of an open playground to signify the Motherland. Youth and boys of all ages engage in a variety of indigenous games, do exercises, *Suryanamaskar*, and sometimes train in skillfully wielding the 'Danda' (stick). The physical-fitness programmes are followed by group singing of patriotic songs. Then there are discussions on national events and problems facing the country. The day's activity culminates in participants' assembling in orderly rows in front of the flag at a single whistle of the group leader, and reverentially reciting the Sanskrit prayer "*Namaste Sada Vatsale Matrubhoome*" (My salutation to you, loving Motherland). The prayer concludes with the powerful patriotic incantation "Bharat Mata Ki Jai." The Guru

Dakshina is a monetary offering made at the *Bhagwa Dhwaj* once in year by each swayamsevak, according to what he can afford. This money is used for sustaining the overall activity of the Sangh. The daily Shakha activity is augmented by graded training-camps celled 'Sangha Shiksha Varga' at provincial and all-India levels, at regular intervals.

The RSS only allows men as members as it was founded to organise Hindu society and considering the practical limitations of the early 20th century. True to the organiastion's progressive nature, when Smt Lakshmibai Kelkar, a social worker from Wardha in Maharashtra approached RSS founder Dr Hedgewar and informed him about the need for similar organization for Hindu women, after holding extensive consultations with him, the Rashtra Sevika Samiti was launched in the year 1936. The objectives of RSS and Samiti are the same and women can join the Rashtra Sevika Samiti as members. As required, RSS and Samiti members work together on assigned projects and activities.

The other false propaganda that is being spread is that RSS does not permit Christians or Muslims as members. The RSS firmly believes that Christians and Muslims of India do not hail from foreign lands but are from our Motherland. At some point of time in history their ancestors changed their religion and ways of worship but that does not separate them from the Hindu society in the larger context or their origins. A large number of Christians and Muslims have been and continue to take an active part in RSS activities with growing interest and increased membership.

SIMPLE STRUCTURE, DEMOCRATIC LEADERSHIP

Guruji Golwalkar had written that the Sangh never entertained the idea of building an organisation as a distinct and separate unit within society. Right from its inception the Sangh has clearly marked out as its goal the moulding of the whole of society, and not merely any one part of it, into an organised entity. That is the reason for the Sangh workers not parading themselves as a 'Sangh group' before the people even when thousands of them work staking their all in times of national catastrophes like famines, floods, flow of refugees from Pakistan, etc. They are content to remain as ordinary members of society and thereby put an example of how even a common man should behave in an alert and organised social life. Such a well-knit, patriotic and self-sustaining national life alone can fortify the nation with overwhelming and everlasting strength, was Guruji's view.

For all that many spread lies that the RSS wants to dominate and control society, it is anything but true, for Guruji always believed that the powerful groups in a society bring with it grave perils to a free and prosperous national growth. In Guruji's words, "We have witnessed such bodies shooting up like meteors on the political horizon in Germany, in Italy, in Russia and China and establishing totalitarian regimes in their respective countries. It is in the nature of these totalitarian parties to seek to perpetuate their domination on society and to enslave people politically, economically, socially, culturally, and in all other respects. The hair-raising reports of mass purges, brainwashing and slave camps that are going on in Russia and China give us a picture of the state of affairs in such countries. The nation's free expression is thereby choked. The individual is annihilated. And bereft of individual initiative and freedom, the society begins to degenerate. The idea of domination through brute strength is absolutely alien to our culture and tradition."

The structure of RSS is simple and with the *swayamsevak* at the base, has positions that are decided upon through democratic processes. The lifestyle of leaders too is very simple and they are given only a frugal honorarium and no salary.

Sarsanghchalak: He is the topmost leader of the RSS and is revered and respected as 'Friend, Philosopher and Guide' by all. Since 1925, the RSS has had Six Sarsanghchalaks from its Founder

Dr Hedgewar to the present incumbent Dr Mohan Madhukar Bhagwat.

Sarkaryawah: Though there no equivalent term in English, the nearest equivalent could be General Secretary. He is the Executive Head of the organisation and conducts the affairs of the Sangh.

Sah-Sarkaryawah: The Joint General Secretary. There can be more than one Sah-Sarkaryawah. At present there are four Sah-Sarkaryawah to assist the Sarkaryawah in conducting the affairs of the Sangh.

Pracharak: An individual who is inspired by the mission and objective of the Sangh and dedicates his full time to carry forward this mission is known as Pracharak in the RSS parlance. He is not someone who publicises or markets the Sangh but is a full time, committed worker with no household attachments, and is akin to a sanyasin.

Mukhya-Shikshak: Incharge head of a Shakha.

Karyawah: Executive head of a shakha.

Gatanayak: A group leader.

Swayamsevak: Selfless volunteer.

Bhagwa Dhwaj: Saffron Flag. RSS has accepted Saffron Flag as its "GURU".

The flag reminds *swayamsevaks* of the glorious history of the nation and the heroic deeds of the countless worthy sons and daughters of India inspiring them to devote their time and energy to serve the society.

The formal structure is only for better organization and functioning of the Sangh so that responsibilities can be allocated and it is not that anyone is superior to the other. An ordinary swayamsevak is as important as Sarsanghachalak or Sarkaryavah.

According to the RSS Constitution:

"Swayamsevak

1. (a) Any male Hindu of 18 years or above, who subscribes to the Aims and Objects of the Sangh and conforms generally to its

discipline and associates himself with the activities of the Shakha will be considered as a Swayamsevak.

(b) A Swayamsevak shall be deemed to be an Active Swayamsevak if he pledges to devote himself for the furtherance of the Aims and Objects of the Sangh, and attends a Shakha regularly or performs any work duly assigned to him.

(c) A Swayamsevak shall cease to be a Swayamsevak if he resigns or is removed for any act prejudicial to the interests of the Shakha or Sangh.

2. Bal-Swayamsevak- Any male Hindu below the age of 18 may be admitted and allowed to participate in shakha programmes as a Bal-Swayamsevak.

Pracharaks

(a) (i) Pracharaks shall be full time workers selected from amongst those devoted workers of high integrity, whose mission is to serve the Society through the Sangh and who, of their own free will, dedicate themselves to the Cause.

(ii) They will receive no remuneration. However their expenses will be met by the Shakhas.

(b) Appointment of Pracharaks.

(i) The Sarkaryavaha will appoint Kshetra and Prant Pracharaks on the advice of the Akhil Bharatiya Pracharak Pramukh and in consultation with the KSHETRA Sanghachalak and Prant Sanghachalak respectively.

(ii) The Prant Sangchalak, on the advice of Prant Pracharak, will appoint Pracharaks for different areas in the Prant for the assistance and co-ordination of the Shakhas in their respective areas.

Sarkaryavaha

(a) The elected members of the Akhil Bharatiya Pratinidhi Sabha (vide Article 15 (a) shall elect the Sarkaryavaha.

(b) The Sarkaryavaha shall act in consultation with the Sarsanghachalak.

(c) The Sarkaryavaha, in consultation with the A.B.K.M.; may constitute a new Pram or Prants, out of existing Prant or Prams Similarly the Sarkaryavaha in consultation with the A.B.K.M.; may constitute a Kshetra comprising of two or mare Prams.

(d) The Sarkaryavaha, in consultation with the Sarsanghachalak, as the case may be, and also the Kshetriya Karyakari Mandal (Ksh. KM.), the Prantiya Karyakari Mandal (Pl(rvi) on an ad hoc basis, all the Kshetra Sanghchalak or Pram Sanghachalak is elected according to the provisions of the Constitution. After the election of the Kshetra or the Pram Sanghachalak, he will form the respective Karyakari Mandal according to the provisions of the Constitution.

(e) The Sarkaryavaha may also nominate additional office bearers of the A.B.K.141.; with specific assignments.

Delegates and Sanghachalaks

(a) (i) Swayamsevaks entitled to vote in a Shakha will elect from among themselves one for every fifty such Swayamsevaks as delegates of the Shakha.

(ii) Swayamsevaks entitled to vote in such of the Shakhas as are having less than fifty such Swayamsevaks, will come together to elect delegates.

(b) The elected members of the Akhil Bharatiya Pratinidhi Sabha vide Art. 15 (a) will elect the concerned Kshetra Sanghachalak.

(c) The delegates, elected as in Art. 16 (a) in a jilla, in a Vibhag and in a Prant will elect the Jilla Sanghachalak, the Vibhag Sanghachalak and the Prant Sanghachalak, respectively.

(d) The Jilla Sanghachalak, in consultation with the Prant Sanghachalak and Pram Pracharak, will nominate Sanghachalaks for the various Shakhas and groups of Shakhas within the Jilla.

(e) In case a suitable person is not available for the office of the Sanghachalak, the Jilla Sanghachalak will appoint a Karyavaha.

1. In case of death, incapacity or resignation of Kshetra, Pram, Vibhag or Jilla Sanghachalak, the K.M. of the larger area may appoint a person to discharge the duties of the respective Sanghachalak until such time as his successor is elected.

(b) The Sanghachalak of a Shakha appointed in accordance with 16 (d) will form a Karyakari Mandal of which he shall be the Chairman, consisting of the following office-bearers duly appointed by him.

(i) Karyavaha

(ii) Shareerik Shikshan Pramukh

(iii) Bouddhik Shikshan Pramukh

(iv) Prachar Pramukh

(v) Vyavastha Pramukh

(vi) Seva Pramukh

(vii) Nidhi Pramukh.

Note: In case suitable persons is/are not available for appointment to any one or more of the above posts the same may remain vacant until suitable person/s is/are available.

(c) Each Karyakari Mandal shall also have in addition not more than five members chosen from amongst the other KARYAKARI Mandals within its area, if any.

(d) K.Ms. will be executive bodies in their respective area, guided by the K.M. of the immediate larger area for implementing the policy and carrying out the programmes laid down by A.B.P.S.

(e) The K.M. of a Shakha will have the power to take disciplinary action against any individual Swayamsevak for breach of discipline or behaviour prejudicial to the interests of the Shakha or the Sangh. Such an action will be subject to confirmation by the KARYAKARI Mandal of the immediate larger area."

SELECTION OF LEADERS BY DEMOCRATIC PROCESS

The process is based on the RSS Constitution that active swayamsevaks in the Shakhas elect their representatives, who further elect their provincial representatives. In proportion to those Prant level representatives, national representatives are elected. These elected members are called Pratinidhis.

Along with Pratinidhis, Prant Sanghachalaks, Prant Pracharaks and all the mentioned office bearers constitute the Electoral College. The election takes place as per the prescribed process. A name is proposed after considering everyone's will and then it is seconded by others.

All positions are selected by through consensus among swayamsevaks and it is they who propose names, before internal elections. When asked in an interview to the Organiser as to how Sangh manages and coordinates with so many of its affiliate organizations, Bhagwat ji said this is something that just happens. "The samskars, actions and goals of swayamsevaks are the only common things. If these three things are there, then coordination and complementarities naturally take place. We just ensure that originality of the swayamsevaks remains intact. Rest of the things take care of themselves. Sangh coordinates even with those people who are not directly Sangh swayamsevaks, but share the same qualities."

With regard to organizational work, Bhagwat ji added that whatever is necessary for the purposes of organisational work is being used. Swayamsevaks used to earlier travel on foot, and then vehicles were provided. He recalls the time when the Sangh had just one vehicle in all of Nagpur, and this was kept for Guruji's use. Maybe three or four Swayamsevaks those days had cars or motorcycles and for most others the bicycle was the most affordable vehicle. Today, many swayamsevaks have vehicles and this is a normal process, he said. "We make sure that we do not become slaves of these comforts and the side-effects of them do not enter the organization," he said.

Bhagwat ji has said that some discipline is important in the building of an individual (*vyakti nirman*) and so a sarsanghchalak is the head of the organization but decision making is a collective process where a new recruit too could express his views freely and it is heard.

THE PRACHARAK'S ORGANISATIONAL SKILLS

At all levels of the RSS structure, the competencies of organizational management and consensus building are important. In this regard, it is interesting to see the how the humble Pracharak, a dedicated swayamsevak who has no household attachments and works full time for the Sangh, plays a key role in affiliate organizations as well as at the political level. The Pracharak is a person skilled in people management and negotiation.

Right from the start, the Pracharak has been a vital resource for the RSS. The exceptional Deendayal Upadhyaya ji was a dedicated Pracharak who was sent s a resource to Dr Syama Prasad Mookerjee when the Bharatiya Jan Sangh was founded.

For its nearly 40 affiliate organisations, RSS nominates at least one of its pracharaks as Sangathan Mantri who works as a general secretary. While Prime Minister Narendra Modi ji was a Pracharak earlier, he was a Sangathan Mantri who wished to continue in politics. Manohar Lal Khattar, Chief Minister of Haryana, and Chief Minister of Uttarakhand Shri Trivendra Singh Rawat were RSS pracharaks.

There are many ministers in the Central government today who were formerly Pracharaks—such as Union Health Minister J.P. Nadda and Petroleum Minister Dharmendra Pradhan.

CHAPTER 3

Sewa Karya—The Heart and Soul of RSS

The RSS's roots in ancient Vedic Hindu culture where service to humanity equals service to God puts Sewa Karya—Service—at the core of the organisation's belief and work.

It is the nature of the service through selfless volunteers or swayamsewaks who are from the society they serve and who do not seek publicity or remuneration that makes RSS Sewa Karya truly unique. Much of the service to persons in need goes unrecorded and it is the person who receives assistance who experiences the Sewa Bhaav—the emotion of service.

When people of all communities are rescued by RSS workers during floods, earthquakes and disasters, and they experience the care with no strings attached or no discrimination, they see the real spirit of the RSS.

DID YOU KNOW?

- Under Rashtriya Sewa Bharti, there are 942 affiliated organizations covering all areas of human life.
- RSS is unparalleled in sheer breadth of coverage with over 1,74,419 projects all across India touching the lives of the most deserving (as of May 2018).
- Sewa Bharti runs 25,136 projects in Education, 89,926 projects in Health, 38,909 in Social Service, rescue and rehabilitation after disasters, 21,975 in Women's Empowerment. The projects keep growing.
- For example, Vanvasi Kalyan Ashram set up in 1952 for supporting

tribal communities in difficult to reach areas has the largest footprint among such organizations in India. The programmes (schools, hostels, libraries health centres, vocational training) are located in 312 districts across India. These are managed by over 1000 full-time workers.

- You might have, sometime in your life, bought a handicraft item made through training from Sangh efforts. Hundreds of girls and women from North Eastern states trained by Sewa Bharti, are successful in the cottage industries of fabric painting, jute work, bamboo craft, embroidery, etc.
- Apart from a basic honorarium to cover expenses at work, the Swayamsevaks are not paid salaries. The work they do for our people is pure Sewa.

"Needy persons must be served with a feeling of brotherhood after understanding their anguish and weakness. Service done with such feelings always bear good results," Suresh Bhaiyaji Joshi, Sarkaryavah (general secretary, RSS), had said in 2018.

Commenting on the marketing of community service done by other organizations, he had said that just as while working for our family members we do not employ propaganda tactics because we consider it as our duty, so too is work done by RSS volunteers.

The RSS was formed to unite and organize Hindus and in the tumultuous times of the decades before Independence, nationalism and protection of Hindus from attacks by Muslims was a priority. After Independence, the organization saw the desperate needs of marginalized populations that were not being considered by most of the new ruling elite from the Congress party. It was often quipped that the English had ensured the creation of a bureaucracy so much like them through Westernised education that they were now the brown sahibs. Many educated politicians of the time, right from India's first Prime Minister Jawaharlal Nehru, were part of the same Westernised ideology, far removed from the economic and cultural realities of the country.

It was when Balasaheb Deoras ji, who was general secretary of the RSS in 1965 and then after the passing of second RSS Sarsangchalak

Guruji Golwalkar, became RSS's third Sarsanghachalak in 1973, that the Sangh focus on Sewa got strong emphasis. Shri Deoras ji was a visionary and believed swayamsevaks should reach out to the people in need all across the country irrespective of caste, religion and socio-economic status. Service or Sewa then became the core of RSS. Volunteers who start with the Sangh since childhood/adolescence go on to either lead a householder's life while still serving people when required or remain unmarried so that the mission of the organization can be carried forward without any compulsions of family life and therefore likely corruption.

Each volunteer of the Sangh is devoted to service related activities. Sewa Bharti is the organization that manages service related activities. Different state units had been working to serve the people right since expansion of RSS some years after its inception. The organization was formally registered as a Public Trust in 2003 as Rashtriya Sewa Bharati in order to efficiently coordinate the activities of all the state units. Social reformers like Swami Vivekananda are the inspiration behind the selfless service. Sewa Bharti is guided by the social service ideology of RSS. Different state units of Sewa Bharati have been working on various social welfare activities for the socially and economically weaker sections of society all over India. The Akhil Bharatiya Saha Seva Pramukh of the RSS guides the organization and is also represented in the Akhil Bharatiya Pratinidhi Sabha, the highest decision making body of the RSS and its affiliates.

It is instructive to note that the biased English media and many urban residents ignorant of the RSS's work mock at the shakhas and paint them as places where workers are taught to hate non-Hindus. It is anything but. In fact, it is due to the swayamsevaks' extensive physical training in the shakhas, that each sangh worker is fully equipped to conduct rescue operations with a quickly deployed team with almost military-like precision. This was seen in the Kerala floods in August 2018 where it was the RSS which reached out to help people and save lives before anyone else. And yet, with a hostile Communist government in power at the state and a biased national media, most of the work of the RSS never got its due. The largest number of relief camps in Kerala, after those run by the state government were set up by the RSS.

RSS through affiliate organizations, has several projects all over the country benefitting millions of people. Most people who are dependent only on a biased media to provide them news are not aware of the sheer volume and scale of RSS activities. Neither does RSS announce its projects and successes nor does it seek any publicity.

Interestingly, if we compare the membership and footprint of the Jesuits, who are considered the largest single order of priests and Brothers in the Catholic Church, with the RSS, some facts emerge. Estimates from writers who study the area say that the Jesuits have seen their numbers decline in recent decades. From when the Society had a total membership of 28,038, of which 20,205 were priests, it saw a 41.5% decline as on 2016 when it had 16,378 members, 11,785 priests and 4,593 Brothers and scholastics. The Jesuits were very active in India in Goa and Southern India and are quite well known among most Indians for their school system. But they only have around 400 schools across India compared to RSS with 12,000 schools and over 32 lakh students!

Comparative Table of Footprint of Jesuits and RSS in India

Sl. No.	Criterion	Society of Jesus – (members called Jesuits)	RSS – India
1.	Membership of volunteers	International- 16,378 members, 11,785 priests and 4,593 brothers and scholastics	58,967 Shakhas. Informal membership close to 9 million
2.	Schools in India	400	12,000
3.	Projects in Adivasi and tribal regions in India	Estimate a few 100 projects*	Over 19,000 projects by Bharaitya Vanvasi Kalyan Ashram in operation

*Complete data of nationwide projects not available

The RSS per se does not get involved in any other activities other than holding daily shakha and arranging various training camps for the Swayamsevaks. As Dr Hedgewar used to say, the RSS is like a powerhouse that generates electric power and transmits it to various establishments. In the same way, the trained RSS Swayamsevaks, according to their inclinations and choice, have been active in various sectors of our social and national life and launched their own initiatives with their feet firmly grounded to their moorings. As of today there are 40-plus such major organisations at national level and numerous such organisations and institutions at state, region and local level.

In order to give an idea of the workings of these organizations, I have tried to describe a few major organizations and the outstanding work they do.

Activities of key organizations like Vanvasi Kalyan Ashram, Vidya Bharti, Ekal Vidyalay, Rashtra Sevika Samiti, Bharatiya Kisan Sangh, Bharatiya Mazdoor Sangh, Disaster Response and Rehabilitation and Vivekananda Kendra are listed below:

BHARATIYA VANVASI KALYAN ASHRAM—SEWA IN THE FORESTS

After Independence on 15 August 1947, and the reins of power passing into the hands of a staunch Fabian Socialist like Nehru, it was clear there would be a strong Communist slant in government functioning. The biggest concern of the RSS then was that Nehru and Congress politicians close to him were Westernised to the point of being ignorant about the hundreds of unique tribal and forest communities in India, and cared little about preserving their culture. Right since the late 19th and early 20th century, these areas had been seeing a lot of Christian missionary activity that had led to deprived communities being induced to convert through the promise of education and employment (this process of inducement and mass conversion is still going on all over India). Tribals are an especially vulnerable section of society. They are Hindu and have unique customs and rituals dating back thousands of years. In a way, since they had not been affected by modernity, they were committed to their own rustic identity and celebrated their own talents.

The challenge before independent India and the RSS with regard to tribals was the alienation of the tribals who lived in remote forest areas, but who form an inseparable part of the Hindu society and proselytization amongst them. The RSS believed it required immediate corrective measures. They had all along been a most exploited community and hence convenient for conversion by Christian missionaries who were out on a mission to maximize their numbers through all means, no matter how devious. It is to counter this twin menace of British legacy, that the Vanavasi Kalyan Ashram was founded in 1952 (renamed in 1963 as Bharatiya Vanavasi Kalyan Ashram). The BVKA, now spread over a 100 districts in 21 States, has been striving for the all-round development of the vanavasis, in their own natural surroundings, enabling all their latent potentialities and talents to blossom. Over the decades, the Ashram has succeeded not only in putting a stop to conversions in all its areas of operation, but also in bringing the converts back to the Hindu fold.

Bharatiya Vanvasi Kalyan Ashram (VKA) (http://kalyanashram.org/) is headquartered in Jashpur, in the state of Chhattisgarh and has administrative offices in Mumbai and Delhi. The Ashram was founded by Shri Ramakant Keshav Deshpande, who was also known as Balasaheb Deshpande. He worked with the Orissa State Department of Tribal Welfare, and it was during his appointment by government post-Independence to work in the tribal dominated Jashpur area as Officer for the Tribal Development Scheme, that he saw how the Christian missionaries had nearly taken over the area and converted the very simple tribals through inducements. He was struck to see how their conversion to Christianity had negatively impacted their ancient cultural roots, ensuring they totally disown their rich past and heritage.

Initially, its objective was to counter the spread of Christianity among tribals by offering alternatives to Christian missionary schools. Starting with schools in Raigarh and Surguja districts, the Ashram grew rapidly. A permanent office was established in 1963, inaugurated by then RSS Sarsangchalak Guruji Golwalkar.

The organization acquired national status during the brief Janata Party government in 1977, and a modified name, Bhəratiya Bhəratiya Vanavasi Kalyan Ashram. Thereafter the organization saw an increase in karyakartas. From 1978 to 1983, full-time karyakartas increased from 44 to 264 (56 of whom were tribal). In the headquarters Jashpur, apart from a hospital, schools, hostels, and training centres were also established in 40 villages. Currently, 312 districts throughout India see the excellent work of the Bharatiya Vanvasi Kalyan Ashram (BVKA) with over 1000 full-time karyakartas. Most of these districts have primary schools, and others have residential schools (*more about Ekal Vidyalay in a later section*), libraries, hostels and health centres. Annually and periodically, events such as medical camps, traditional sports events and tribal festivals are celebrated.

The organization focuses on the welfare activities of *Janjatis* (Scheduled Tribes), Vanvasis and Adivasis (forest dwellers) in the remotest areas of India. Its branches across India work with tribal communities to improve healthcare, education of children, farming output and enhancing sporting abilities. VKA also works in creating cultural awareness among *janjatis* so that they internalize the idea of preservation of their unique tradition and customs, feel pride in it and do not fall prey to Christian missionary conversion.

Tu-Main Ek Rakt (You-Me of One Blood) is the motto of this organization. Here again, it is the selfless sewa of the swayamsevaks that ensures support reaches the tribals in need. Over 19,000 projects are in operation. Along with karyakartas who actually work in the deep forest areas, there are thousands of karyakartas in urban areas as well. They render their support for fulfilling the organisation's objectives in ensuring justice in terms of laws related to protection of forest dwellers and ensuring no encroachment of vital forest land.

A PROUD WOMAN POLICE COMMANDO FROM NAGALAND

Ms Chiewelou Thele, Delhi Police.

The woman police officer who graces one of the posters of Delhi Police commandos, holding an AK-47, is a true example of courage and commitment. Ms Chiewelou is a resident of Masulumi village in Fek district of Nagaland. Her mother is in the Nagaland Police and brother is in the Indian Army. Many of her relatives are also in the Police and Army.

Chiewelou came to Shabari Kanya Ashram (Vanvasi Kalyan Ashram, Raipur, Chhattisgarh) in class 6, in order to get a good education. Teachers recall her as a student quite different from her peers. When anyone asked about her objective in life, she always said, "I have to join the Police and serve the country." In school, she was a Girl Guide, and always used to do her best in competitions well.

After completing her education, Chiewelou applied for the Delhi Police and was selected.

Senior police say Chiewelou was chosen to be the face of Delhi Police, because she was the best trainee of her batch. "I had never even seen a rifle before joining the police force, but I am the best female shooter of my batch, and the credit goes to my archery training," she said.

Chhev, who was very fond of archery in her school days, made best use of the facilities and training available in Vanvasi Kalyan Ashram as well as the encouragement from teachers. She went on to win many national level archery competitions

Chiewelou says, "I was craving to be photographed when I was younger but now you can realize my happiness by knowing that people will see me in the entry of the Commandos on all the posters of Delhi Police. It is not possible to describe happiness in words."

VIDYA BHARATI AKHIL BHARATIYA SHIKSHA SANSTHAN—SEWA IN EDUCATION

It is the RSS through this organization that runs the largest private school network in India (12,000 with over 32 lakh students) that enables students to have a complete understanding of their identity and cultural traditions in addition to subjects as per Board Curriculum.

Headquartered in Lucknow, Uttar Pradesh, Vidya Bharti has a functional office in Delhi and a sub-office in Kurukshetra, Haryana.

The history of Vidya Bharti is interesting and points to an intolerance to Hindu cultural roots by the Westernised ruling elite immediately after independence. It was in 1946 that a Gita school was established in Kurukshetra under the initiative of RSS Sarsangchalak Guruji Golwalkar. An unfair ban on RSS after the assassination of Mahatma Gandhi in 1948 by Nathuram Godse (who was not a member of RSS but was proclaimed by Congress and Communists as being so), led to the Gita School initiative taking a backseat.

The first Saraswati Shishu Mandir school was set up by RSS in Gorakhpur in 1952 by Nanaji Deshmukh, a committed social activist who went on to become one of the noted leaders of the Bharatiya Jan Sangh. This school model caught on fast among the people and as the number of schools increased, a *Shishu Shiksha Prabandak Samiti* (committee), was set up to coordinate activities at state-level. Schools and committees were set up in Delhi, Bihar, Madhya Pradesh and Andhra Pradesh. With schools expanding exponentially, the need was felt from among the RSS in 1977-78 for an all-India body, to coordinate all education activities.

Thus Vidya Bharati, headquartered in Delhi, was constituted to coordinate activities of all the state committees. Vidya Bharati was a professional body and had an associated National Academic Council that consisted of a range of educationists, not just those affiliated with the Sangh, and was recognized by the National Council of Educational Research and Training (NCERT).

It was the sub-optimal education offered by state schools that led to the growth of Vidya Bharti-run schools. The Vidya Bharti schools had grown to 5,000 in number by the early 1990s and today, the Vidya Bharti network stands at 12,000 schools with over 32 lakh students, with close to one lakh teachers. Most of the schools are affiliated to the Central Board for Secondary Education (CBSE) or the respective State School Boards. It would be correct to say that the growth in Vidya Bharti run schools co-incided with the Janata Party coming to power at the Centre in 1977 in which Bharatiya Jan Sangh was an ally. This unshackled the stranglehold of sub-par schooling in India and an education devoid of our Hindu cultural base that was being imparted to children in state schools.

> Today, schools in Britain are teaching Sanskrit to English children, as was reported in the media some months ago, and many European countries are encouraging children to learn Sanskrit since it is seen as the most scientific language and of great use in Artificial Intelligence, which is the future of technology.
>
> And here, in India, the very birthplace of this greatest of all languages—Sanskrit—there continues to be opposition to teach it in the name of secularism!

The formal schools are called Shishu Vatikas, Shishu Mandirs, Vidya Mandir, Saraswati Vidyalas, as applicable, and Vidya Bharati also runs sanskar kendras (cultural schools) as well as single-teacher schools for cultural education. Over 250 intermediate colleges and 25 institutions of higher education and training colleges also come under the institution. Its schools operate out o north-eastern states which are quite remote from the mainland and are hence underserved, in addition to southern Indian states.

Underdeveloped regions especially those with tribal communities are a special focus of Vidya Bharti. Funds for operational expenses are collected through various means like voluntary contributions and from charities across the world. It is instructive to note that strong attempts were made by organizations like Vidya Bharti to Indianise our educational system after Independence and free it from the shackles of Lord Macaulay (who realized that Indian civilization was ancient and stable and the only way to break the back of such civilized people is enforce English medium education and create a set of elite that are disconnected from their roots). But they were met with resistance from Indians themselves!

But true success speaks for itself. In 2016, Assam state Board results, not only was the state topper, Sarfaraz, from a Vidya Bharti school, he was one of 44 candidates of Vidya Bharati-affiliated schools in the Top 20 ranking students that year. The newspaper (text below) chooses to highlight "Muslim" but for Vidya Bharti, all its students are equal.

ASSAM CLASS 10 TOPPER IS A MUSLIM BOY FROM RSS-BACKED SCHOOL

A Muslim boy has given the RSS in Assam a reason to rejoice again, a week after a BJP-led government came to power in the state for the first time.

Jun 01, 2016

Digambar Patowary
Hindustan Times

A Muslim boy has given the RSS in Assam a reason to rejoice again, a week after a BJP-led government came to power in the state for the first time.

Sarfaraz Hussain topped the state board's Class 10 exam with 590 marks out of a maximum 600. The results were declared on Tuesday.

Others before him have had similar scores. But 16-year-old Sarfaraz is the first Muslim to pass from a school run by an affiliate of Vidya Bharati, the RSS's education wing.

He is not the only Muslim student of Sankardev Sishu Niketan, one of the many schools run by the Vidya Bharati-affiliated Sishu Shiksha Samiti, Assam. The school at Betkuchi on the outskirts of Guwahati has 24 Muslim students, most of whom—like Sarfaraz—have won prizes for reciting the Bhagwad Gita.

"They have never complained about what we teach because our emphasis is on academic excellence apart from giving the students a grip on Indian culture and values," Akshaya Kalita, the school's headmaster, told HT.

"We did not make them feel different, and as a rule, they have lunch with all the other students and teachers after a bhojan mantra (prayer before meal)," he said.

Ajmal Hussain, Sarfaraz's father, said he let his son study in the school because it provided free education. "It would have otherwise been difficult to sustain his studies with my meagre income as a waiter in a small restaurant," he said. He credited his son's success to his hard work, the support from his schoolteachers, and also to the Hindu goddess of learning, Saraswati. Sarfaraz was the secretary of the school's Saraswati Puja celebrations.

"The school shaped my life, and I hope to achieve greater academic glory as my teachers expect," Sarfaraz said, wishing he could repay his alma mater some day.

State secondary board officials said of the 381,585 students that appeared for this year's Class 10 exam, 239,614 passed to clock a 62.79% success rate. Sarfaraz was one of 44 candidates of Vidya Bharati-affiliated schools in the Top 20.

Vidya Bharati in 1998 during a conference of Indian State education ministers, presented proposals for school education to be "Indianized, nationalized and spiritualized," with the teaching of "the essentials of Indian culture." When the Uttar Pradesh government made it mandatory for children in school to start their day by singing Saraswati Vandana (invocation to the Goddess of Learning, Devi Saraswati) and Vande Mataram (the National Song), this was perceived as "Hindu education" and Muslim organizations stopped Muslim school children from singing them. Another proposal from Vidya Bharati was that Sanskrit be taught in all schools and to revise textbooks so that relevant Hindu examples were provided in subjects instead of foreign names. Today, schools in Britain are teaching English children Sanskrit, as was reported in the media some months ago, and many European countries are encouraging children to learn Sanskrit since it is seen as the most scientific language and of great use in Artificial Intelligence, which is the future of technology. And here, in India, the very birthplace of this greatest of all languages, Sanskrit, there continues to be opposition in the name of secularism!

Dinanath Batra, former General Secretary of Vidya Bharati, said that they were fighting an "ideological battle against Macaulay,

Marx and Madarasawadis." Vidya Bharati maintains that it advocates "Indianization, nationalization and spiritualization" of education. Aside from the core curriculum, in areas like music and cultural education and physical training, the organisation worked out its own curriculum and techniques.

EKAL VIDYALAYA FOUNDATION (FOUNDATION OF SOLO SCHOOLS)

"If the poor child cannot go to school, the school must come to him,"

– Swami Vivekananda

Though not under Vidya Bharti, a mention must be made of the truly unique Sewa model of the Ekal Vidyalaya, a much awarded initiative, working in rural and tribal areas. These are single-teacher based schools, working on the principle of "Ek Shikshak, Ek Vidyalaya" (One teacher for every school). There are a whopping 76,611 Ekal Vidyalayas educating over 20 lakh children in remote and tribal areas. Typically, in remote areas where state machinery has not reached, there are no school buildings and neither are there teachers. The individual schools, are called Ekal Vidyalayas and have local teachers who teach in the regional language or dialect using different techniques like dramas, folk stories and songs. Children are also trained in moral education, healthcare and organic farming. The lack of a building or infrastructure does not deny these children the right to a holistic education.

The Ekal Vidyalaya Foundation (EVF) was established in 1986 by Rakesh Popli (late), a US-returned Indian nuclear scientist, and his wife, a child education specialist along with other specialists, with support from the Vishwa Hindu Parishad, an RSS affiliate organization. On the Ekal website, it is stated that the Ekal Movement today stands on the strong foundation built by many leaders and Volunteers at different levels. Indeed this is the Sewa Bhaav that I mentioned in the first part of this chapter.

Ekal Vidyalay Foundation grew from strength to strength and Bharat Lok Shiksha Parishad was formed in 2000 to develop chapters in north India with its headquarters in Delhi. Currently Bharat Lok Shiksha Parishad has 12 chapters in north India. This organization also helps promote cultural heritage through ethics and value education as well as establish mobile cultural centres in remote villages.

In the year 2008, Ekal Sansthan was formed to support Ekal Abhiyan in research and development, communication strategies, training and capacity building of volunteers, strategic interventions, and to create avenues in urban areas to bridge the gap between rural and urban communities.

Swami Vivekananda's words are the inspiration for EVF – "We want the education by which character is formed, strength of mind is increased, the intellect is expanded, and by which one can stand on one's own feet."

ONE TEACHER SCHOOL

It was the experience of the EVF founders of running schools in tribal areas of Gumla district in Jharkhand and night schools for tribal people in Orissa that helped evolve the concept of One Teacher School.

At a seminar organised to find out the solution to the problem of rampant illiteracy in tribal villages, the concept of "One Teacher Schools" was conceived of formally in Gumla. Models from Jharkhand and Orissa were discussed and seen as a way forward. Bhau Rao Devras, a renowned social activist and brother of RSS Sarsangchalak Balasaheb Deoras, had outlined the concept of One Teacher School. Dr. Rakesh Popli helped in refining the concept and wrote the Book "Khele Kude Nache Gaye" about non-formal methods of teaching.

The process of setting up an Ekal Vidyalay is fairly straightforward. Ekal Vidyalaya is established in a village once a Gram Samiti is formed and takes the responsibility to monitor and support the EV's activities. It is only then that there is local ownership and involvement of the village community in the EV.

Thereby, the EV provides five-fold education in a village for children as well as the entire village community including rural women, rural youth, farmers and panchayat members.

The primary objective of EV is to enable functional literacy among children in the village. The EV runs usually for three hours a day and six days a week and has an average of 30 students. As students are admitted after an assessment of their literacy level, three groups are formed to optimize teaching. Thereby they learn basic skills of reading, writing, basic arithmetic, general science and basic social study.

Health care awareness is another key objective of teaching so that there is awareness among children and village community about health and hygiene. This is done through demonstrations of best practices, and reinforcing the importance of sanitation in the village so that a large part of basic healthcare needs is addressed. Nutrition advice is also given to the older community members during the weekly Vidyalay. In addition, students are trained on Development Education including organic farming, Empowerment Education (so that they know important laws that concern them and about Government welfare programmes) and Ethics and Value Education.

ATTACKED FOR DOING GOOD?

The EVF has come in for unwanted criticism in the past from international organizations supporting Christian missionaries who say the EVs teach Hindu cultural education so that the tribals do not convert to other religions. One could naturally ask if anything is wrong in an organization imparting the national and cultural values of its own country so that its vulnerable populations and their unique way of life are not exploited? Wouldn't any country do the same? Why then are Hindus and India held accountable to a yardstick that is unfair and discriminatory?

EVF suffered a blow in May 2005 when the Indian government (UPA I led by Congress Party) stopped grants to the schools based a report prepared by an enquiry committee of the Ministry of Human

Resource Development that said it found that in some Ekal Vidyalaya schools the names of enrolled students had been copied from registers of Government schools. It added that the schools did not provide reading and learning material, and used funds to "generate hatred toward minorities, and condition the minds of children." The report pointed to misuse of funds, and using the grants for creating disharmony amongst religious groups and creating a political cadre.

This was despite the fact that a good number of independent reports had come out documenting the success achieved by Ekal Vidyalaya. Studying the non-formal education experiment by EVF in Jharkhand from 1986 to 1995–96, Digital Learning, an premier education magazine, described the Ekal Vidyalay as "extraordinary," noting that literacy rate in Jharkhand doubled in this period, and diseases caused by unhygienic practices, witchcraft and alcoholism declined sharply. The National Rural Health Mission too has availed of the support of Ekal Vidyalay Foundation to expand outreach in tribal areas.

RASHTRA SEVIKA SAMITI—WOMEN POWER

The RSS had taken birth in 1925 and Indian women were taking part in the freedom struggle in their own capacity. The RSS was restricted to male members, given the dangers of the time and the critical requirement of strengthening and uniting the Hindu community. It was in the 1930s that the mother of a Maharashtrian RSS swayamsevak, Smt Lakshmibai Kelkar, also known as 'mausiji', approached RSS Founder and Sarsangchalak Dr Hegdewar, several times in the early 1930s to request him to admit women into the RSS. In 1936, Dr Hedgewar, with all his foresight, advised her to set up a separate unit for women. The Rashtra Sevika Samiti was thus formed with aims similar to the RSS viz, training women about their cultural roots and responsibilities in individual and societal development.

Rashtra Sevika Samiti was started in 1936 at Wardha by Lakshmibai Kelkar (Mousiji). The Samiti believes that woman is nature itself, the primordial power of the universe. Whatever is visible in this whole world, it is reflected in the influence of the same divine power, therefore it is consciousness. This supremacy is considered as the Goddesses Mahalaxmi, Mahasaraswati, Mahakali and the power of that Parabrahma (Supreme Power). The Samiti believes Indian culture has flowed with inspiration from this concept that every woman is part of that Shaktityatva. The formation of Indian society is seen as a part of the Brahma Chaitanya Shakti, which is woven around the existence of women. In the Gita, Bhagwan Shri Krishna is believed to be the basis of the dormant powers of women for social perception. Awakening the power of that power, uniting the power, the unique goal of putting it into the nation-building work is the basis behind Mousiji establishing the Rashtra Sevika Samiti.

In the 21st Century, there is much talk about Female Power but way back in 1936 the Samiti was formed emphasizing this very fact. The Shakha and Sewa are the base of the Samiti too, and women sevikas are imparted physical training, Yoga, as well as intellectual training on the basic values of Hindi civilization, along with discussions on the same.

The Samiti shakhas spread gradually from Wardha into Rajasthan and Karnataka, and by 1978 the Sevika Samiti had spread all over India. The estimated membership base is 10 lakh women. There are 4,900 shakhas of Rashtra Sevika Samiti (as of 2017). Ma Shanta Kumari is the Pramukh Sanchalika and Ma Sita Gayatri is the Pramukh Karyavahika.

In the Samiti Shakha (local branch), a regular gathering of members meet for one hour where they practice yoga, play games, sing nationalist/patriotic songs, discussions/lectures on nationalistic topics. Rashtra Sevika Samiti focuses on Hindu women's role in the society as leaders and agents of positive social reform. Samiti teaches its members three ideals:

Matrutva (Universal Motherhood), Kartrutva (Efficiency and Social Activism), Netrutva (Leadership).

The Samiti has a significant footprint in *Sewa* with 480 Education projects, 480 Women's Self Help Groups and 45 health initiatives across India. To Samiti members 'sewa" means respecting others. It believes that the selfless service by a woman has a natural quality to it. Through Sewa, the Samiti believes in enlightening the spirit of the nation, its way of life, and culture. The Samiti's Sewa is involved in Swasthya (Health), Shiksha (Education), Samskara (Value Education), Counselling Centres, Hostels and Swavalamban (Self-reliance).

A very good example of the excellent work done by the Samiti is that of the Samskruti Seva Trust in Hubbali, Karnataka. Samskruti Seva Trust is a women's self help group organization in the district. Women from low income groups are selected for this project and are taught income generation activities like Stitching and Training Center, Personality Development Camps, Small Scale Designer Products Manufacturing and Marketing etc. The trust also runs a Holige Kendra to make popular sweets. Products made by the women are marketed by the Trust. The income earned after selling the products are given directly to the women. The women earn money and this increases their self-esteem. The Trust is managed by over 50 volunteers and has trained over 500 women. These women have gone on to earn an income of over Rs 10 lakh by selling products.

BHARATIYA KISAN SANGH—SEWA FOR FARMERS

India is predominantly an agricultural country. Right since the days of subjugation by Mughal invaders and later the British colonizers, the farmers have always been at the receiving end of hostile policies that exploited them and did not give them their due. Such is the unique agricultural bounty of India that the country has over 52% natural arable land all year round without any artificial intervention, as agricultural areas in India see the perfect balance of perennial rivers and the most fertile soil. It is this agricultural richness that has been the source of India's historical wealth and plenty, making it the richest country since thousands of years, thereby attracting invaders including Alexander the Great in ancient times to Mughals and later European colonizers and the British.

Despite the blessings of nature, India began to see a systematic neglect of agriculture and farmers' needs since Independence. After Independence, due to rampant corruption farmers did not get a fair price and faulty distribution of food to the deserving led to famines in the 1950s. India was dependent on the US for wheat imports and this situation was set right only after the Green Revolution of the 1960s which eventually made India self-sufficient in grains.

Farmers were being exploited even worse than when under foreign rule especially with Nehru's economic policies skewed heavily towards industrialisation. Despite many countries in the world seeing development, the Indian village based farmer felt cheated and left out in the pace of development. While other organizations representing farmers did come up after Independence, they either represented powerful individuals and vested interests or were politically affiliated. They used farmers to further their own ambitions. There was a need felt to have a non political organization which could awaken farmers towards creatively achieving their rights and getting their due while not ignoring their duties as citizens of the country.

The Bharatiya Kisan Sangh (BKS) was thus established as an Indian Farmers' Organisation in March 1979 at Kota, Rajasthan where hundreds of workers working for the Kisan in various fields, from all the states of this nation, had assembled. BKS was founded by Shri. Dattopanthji Thengadi, who had founded the Bhartiya Mazdoor Sangh and such organisations previously and was an internationally acclaimed thinker.

Among the main aims and objectives of BKS are:

- To unite and organise the Kisans (farmers) to improve their financial social, cultural, educational, conditions and activities in cottage industries by making available stable avenues of livelihood and survival

- To make available information and other related literature in respect of new innovations, improvements, methodologies etc. in the field of Agriculture Technology and to encourage the Kisan to adopt the same.
- To emphasis to importance and suitability of age old agriculture techniques, methodology and to combine the same with modern inventions so as to have ecological security of fertile soil, adequate water, seeds, cattle, plants and biodiversity.
- To collect, experiment, innovate, improve and publicise the centuries old practices and usages in the agriculture field so as to benefit others as well as to protect the same from being patented.

The BKS's ideology is Krishimit Krushasva (Do Only Farming). It operates with the organizational efficiency of the RSS with committees at village, taluk, district and state level representing farmers. The organisation is non-political and believes that Upliftment of the Farmer is Upliftment of the Rashtra.

Right since inception, seeing the genuine commitment of BKS workers, large number of farmers joined in and the organization expanded rapidly to be present in all states with presence at district level and in some areas including taluk level as well. The membership is estimated at 2 crore. BKS has organized many movements to press for the demands of farmers and follows Constitutional norms. It has been successful in meeting most of farmers' demands and BKS' opinion is respected in terms of farm policy formulation.

Another significant activity that BKS emphasizes on is reviving age-old agricultural techniques and methods and combining the same with modern inventions so as to enable ecological security of fertile soil and preserve biodiversity. This is a critical global requirement today, world over, as barren lands are increasing globally and also in India due to excessive use of chemical pesticides and fertilizers that renders the soil unsuitable for farming. It is an area where India has a unique advantage to become a global knowledge resource for agriculture and organic farming.

The case study below on the Seed Ball Technique represents the BKS' efforts in this regard. This was widely reported by the media over 2017-18 under the activities of NGO Uttishta Bharata which worked with BKS in this regard.

SEED BALL "Transforming and Rejuvenating dry lands, barren lands and manmade deserts of Bharat into forests using Seed Ball Technique"

Lands in India have been orphaned and deserted by people due to many reasons.

Primarily among them being due to excessive use of pesticides and chemical fertilizers, underground seepage of chemical effluents from heavy manufacturing industries which do not treat their effluents and dump them into water sources like streams, rivers and waste lands.

Seed Ball or also called as "Earth Balls" was rediscovered by a Japanese farming pioneer Mr. Masanobu Fukuoka. He implemented this and revived waste lands, into a fertile region covered with thick forests.

The Seed Ball Technique was pioneered in India by **Gangadhar, Secretary of Bharatiya Kisan Sangh**, who vowed to bring back the forests and greenery around the villages surrounding Bangalore.

So what is this "Seed Ball Technique"?

Seeds are placed in the middle of a ball made up of moist mixture of clay, red soil, cow dung and cow urine. The cow dung and urine acts as natural compost and provides microbial inoculants. Then this Seed ball is dried up in shade and becomes hard. This dried, hard Seed ball is then sowed or thrown in waste lands, dry lands, uninhabited lands just before the monsoon or rainy season.

The rains soak the seed ball, the seeping water germinates the seed inside the seed ball. The sprouting seed uses the nutrients of the seed ball and its roots spread inside the land and grows up to become a tree sapling. This sapling grows up to become a big tree. Since the seed struggles for its survival to grow up into a sapling, the sapling adapts to its environment better than those where a grown sapling is planted. Inspired by his commitment and dedication, youth from Uttishta Bharatha, joined hands and made 6000 seed balls in a day. The target is to make 100000 seed balls, which will be planted across the periphery of

Bangalore by school children and youths. Traditionally seed ball was thrown in dry lands, which would grow into forests. In this method, less than 50% of the seed balls survive and grow into tree saplings.

Uttishta Bharatha, with the guidance of Mr. Gangadhar ji, is taking a new approach to ensure that all the seed balls that are sowed grow into tree saplings. For this, we will involve school children and hold Vanamahotsava competition.

Benefits of implementing Seed Ball Technique

- Greenery in dry lands.
- Better oxygen levels and oxygen density in cities, villages and reduced pollution.
- Lower carbon dioxide emissions, as trees absorb them.
- Lower soil Erosion during rainy season.
- Increase in underground water levels.
- Wood, bio mass, and compost for farmers from tree leaves, branches.
- Healthier and Stronger Bharat.

(Parts of an article taken from Bharatiya Kisan Sangh website)

DISASTER RESPONSE

The area of emergency response during disasters is one where even the greatest cynic has been forced to admit the exemplary and selfless service of the karyakartas. All through the length and breadth of the country and Nepal, the RSS swayamsevaks have saved hundreds of thousands of lives right from the Odisha Cyclone of 1971, Andhra Pradesh Cyclone of 1977, the Bhopal Gas Disaster of 1984 to the 2001 Gujarat earthquake, right up till the Kerala Floods of August 2018. Not just that, right from helping Hindu and Sikh refugees fleeing from newly created Pakistan into India post-Partition in August 1947, to helping provide provisions in remote Himalayan regions to Indian soldiers during Indo-China War of 1962, it is the Sangh workers who have been right at the forefront of helping people in distress.

In all the natural calamities, after immediate rescue operations, RSS rebuilt villages, provided shelter for the victims, provided clothes, medicines and sanitary equipment, adopted orphaned children and rehabilitated the victims.

Kerala August 2018

When the sudden floods and its heaviest rains of 10 years struck Kerala in August 2018, there was chaos all around with a state machinery that was unprepared and people caught unawares in the middle of the night.

Almost immediately, 10,000 volunteers of the RSS started rushing to the aid of dangerously stranded flood victims of Kerala, uprooted from their homes. After the Indian Army and Air Force rescue teams were deployed a few days later, the *swayamsevaks* actively participated in combined rescue efforts in all the 14 districts of Kerala. It is estimated that the RSS cadre had rescued 75,600 people during the Kerala floods.

After the waters receded, around 2,00,000 volunteers took part in the clean-up drive in the state on 1 September 2018.

RSS volunteer Rajesh Padmar was quoted then as saying how the organisation has put its plans and preparations in place so that they can serve effectively. He said the volunteers were divided into three teams where one took care of 'direct rescue' - especially in areas where people were stranded by floods or where there had been landslides. Another team of swayamsevaks took care of providing food and shelter, especially in 'Kendriya Vidyalayas' and other schools where many persons had taken refuge. The third team worked on providing medical facilities, medicines, and other essential materials for the rescued persons. Kerala Seva Bharati, a registered body affiliated to the RSS, helped in facilitating people in and around the country to provide monetary help online. Through this we can see how organisational efficiency is embedded at the very foundation of Sewa in RSS and how the years of training by swayamsevaks' makes them the most efficient response teams in times of disaster.

Such is the dedication of swayamsevaks that they risk their own lives to ensure maximum numbers of persons are rescued. At least two swayamsevaks unfortunately lost their lives while saving the lives of people in Kerala after the August 2018 floods.

The list of life-saving support offered by swayamsevaks who see no barriers of caste or creed when they lend a helping hand is very long but a mention is made below of the notable rescue service under Sewa:

- In 2001 Gujarat Earthquake 25,000 swayamsevaks helped save over 20,000 lives.

  In 2004 Tsunami it was swayamsevaks who immediately started working with their bare hands digging through the beaches and debris to save lives and retrieve bodies. Editor of Tughlaq, the noted writer and dramatist Late Cho Ramaswamy, had written then that "The concerned authorities admit privately that it was the RSS-sponsored Sewa Bharati, which did yeoman service everywhere. Politicsforbids them to acknowledge this in public."
- Following the devastating 2013 Uttarakhand floods in the floods and cloudburst that created havoc in Uttarakhand in June 2013, Sewa Bharati had deployed 5,000 RSS swayamsevaks for the relief and rescue operations along with the Indian Armed Forces. It was the largest ever rescue mission for the 100,000 pilgrims and locals. From the first day of floods until the operations continued, 20 truckloads of relief material were sent to flood affected areas from Dehra Dun. RSS Sewa Vibhag surveyed the flood affected areas of Badrinath, Hemkund Saheb, Kedarnath and Gangotri-Yamunotri and found that approximately 200 villages were worst affected by the floods and some of them were completely washed out. The excellent on-ground team efforts by RSS helped saved thousands of lives.

BHARATIYA MAZDOOR SANGH (INDIAN WORKERS ASSOCIATION)

The very terms "Workers Union or Labour Union" conjures up an image of striking workers and an undeniable Communist influence.

But the Bharatiya Mazdoor Sangh, which is estimated to have a membership of 10 million, was founded in July 1955 as a unique, nationalist organization and works as such to ensure the due rights of industry workers, seeing the worker as contributing to the growth of India.

BMS, which is not affiliated to any International Trade Union Confederation, sees the worker as one with all the people of India and does not promote any class divisions and rejects the Marxist ideology of class struggle. For the purpose of membership verification, 44 industries have been classified by the Ministry of Labour, Government of India of which BMS has affiliated unions in all. The organization has a membership of almost 10 million in all states of India comprising more than 5000 affiliate unions.

BMS rejects the idea of State control and views it as an necessary only for areas like defence but stands firmly for public accountability of each industry. Consumers are the third and most important party to industrial relations for the BMS in keeping with the spirit of nationalism and patriotism. The creation of BMS, is epochal in the trade union space as it charted its own unique course. It is noteworthy that while the Communist slogan states, "Workers of the World Unite" BMS slogan says—"Workers, Unite the World."

In an environment rife with mistrust and exploitation of workers, it truly takes vision and remarkable commitment to start a nationalistic organization like Bharatiya Mazdoor Sangh, to address concerns of workers. And the process was not easy.

The idea of a nationalistic non-Marxist workers union in 1955 was only a concept of a few determined swayamsevaks who had assembled in Bhopal under the guidance of Dattopant Thengadi – a noted thinker and intellectual, who had dedicated his entire life to social work. He collected a group of determined workers to work for this idea. Thengadiji was a visionary having instituted Swadeshi Jagran Manch previously as well as one of the founder members of Akhil Bharatiya Vidyarthi Parishad, and then the Bharatiya Kisan

Sangh. Seeing the need for an organization of workers, he conceptualized the Bharatiya Mazdoor Sangh.

Thengadiji was a truly unique Indian nationalist, and remained a full-RSS *pracharak* until his death in October 2004. The impact of his simple living and commitment to nationalist ideals influenced future generations and still does. Interestingly, he even refused to accept the Padma Bhushan Award saying there were more deserving candidates than him. A trained lawyer from Wardha, Maharashtra, he was widely travelled, erudite and well-read, in addition to being an author of books in Marathi and English.

Workers are Part of Society

It must be noted here that while almost all other trade unions formed out of splits in existing trade unions, the BMS was not formed in this manner. Hence, it had to literally build its organisational base right from scratch. It is remarkable that when BMS started, it had no membership and no activists (karyakarta), no office or funding. Right from the start, guided by the zeal of Thengadiji, BMS was defined as a trade union which would be rooted in nationalism, would work as a genuine trade union, and remain apolitical. This stood out because other trade unions were linked to political parties and narrow political interests denied workers their true rights.

Thengadiji and his committed RSS colleagues toured India and set up offices wherever possible. In an already active space, these efforts seemed small in comparison to the well established Unions. Most of these Unions set up by BMS were in the unorganised sector. As BMS gained in strength, Unions came up in a few industries and in a few states, State Committees were also formed.

Finally, 12 years after the formation of BMS, it was in 1967 that the first all India Conference of the organization was held in Delhi, in which the first national executive was elected. Then, the number of affiliated unions was 541 and total membership was 2,46,000.

Thengadiji was elected General Secretary and Ram Nareshji as first President.

For the BMS, national interest is supreme and the workers' interest to be protected and promoted within that framework. Thus, it is national commitment that guides all negotiations and good of the country, the industry and the workers was accepted by members as the guiding principles.

BMS believes that workers are part of the Indian society and have the obligation to serve our society. Consumers' interest is considered akin to national interest and hence the Bhagwa Dhwaj (saffron flag) of BMS, which is a symbol of sacrifice and service, far removed from Communist inspired red flags, began to be seen in the trade union arena. BMS' symbol represents the rhythm between human controlled industrial development and agricultural prosperity, depicted by impression of strong, confident and erect thumb of fist in between a moving wheel and sheaf of corn. Interestingly, BMS is the first among trade unions to use a logo of human organ.

Standing up for Workers who Need Support

Bharatiya Mazdoor Sangh has never shied away from its Sewa to ensure justice to workers. Its successes during Indo-China War (1962) and Bangladesh Liberation war (1971) in mobilizing workers are well known. BMS has advocated impartially for the welfare of workers on issues that other politically affiliated trade unions have ignored.

An interesting example with regard to the **rights of domestic workers** is worth sharing. We might think it is only in the last few years that this issue has gained importance as domestic workers are vulnerable in an unorganized sector. But as far back as 1971, BMS raised the issue and formed a separate union for them. When BMS started working among the unorganised domestic servants of Mumbai (then Bombay), it formed a separate union for them by name "Kharelu Kamgar Sangh." Support for domestic workers was required as contrary to conventional employment, one domestic worker might work with more than one employer, and sometimes even eight to ten different employers. These workers did not have any legal recognition or safeguards in labour laws. Their only security was the new union. In keeping with the BMS philosophy of not indulging in destructive strikes and protests, this union too adopted the method of peaceful satyagraha. A huge rally of around 60,000 Gharelu Kamgar (domestic workers) was organized on the streets of Mumbai on May 22nd and 23rd, 1972 on the third conference of BMS that was held there.

VIVEKANANDA KENDRA

Keeping alive the philosophy of Swami Vivekananda who inspired people from across the world is the Vivekananda Kendra (VK), founded in January 1972 in Kanyakumari, Tamil Nadu by Eknath Ranade ji. It was the relentless efforts of Ranade ji that earlier led to the construction of the Vivekananda Rock Memorial in 1970. It took six years of struggle, including facing opposition from Catholics and resistance from state and national government. It was the unmistakable commitment of Ranadeji that led to the famous Memorial for one of the Greatest Sons of India, which has now become a must-see destination for all.

Swami Vivekananda had said that:

"An aggregate or a congregation of men does not make a nation, nor do the geographical area and duration of time qualify a society to be known as a nation. A government formed on such a basis can be called a state, but not a nation. It is a common goal or mission that makes a nation. All the constituents strive collectively for something noble. Service with spiritual orientation results in man-making which are invariably and inseparably connected with nation building."

It is the core of all the thoughts behind RSS and Vivekananda Kendra. The Kendra takes forward this mission of spiritually oriented Sewa by serving and connecting with people in various ways. It is operational in 21 states of India through 225 branch centres and projects.

Right since it was started, VK has undertaken a large number of service activities in North East India, which was much neglected by the Central Government since Independence.

Awareness of the need of organized work for strengthening of the nation is generated through Karyapaddhati (work) to actualize Swami Vivekananda's vision of Jagadguru Bharat. A committed cadre is created by organizing three stage karyakarta prashikshan shibirs to induct new workers to its cadre every year. Kendra Karyakartas spread Swamiji's message of selfless service and love for India and pride in our own culture through these activities.

A number of camps like Yoga Shibir, Spiritual Retreat, Maitri Shibir, and Personality Development Shibir are also organised at different places.

Swami Vivekananda's Vision was to rebuild India in tune with her personality that was enshrined in yoga and its spiritual base. The genius of Shri Ranadeji focused on the holistic concept of yoga, as another name for spirituality in the very words of Swami Vivekananda—'Each Soul is potentially Divine,'—and adopted yoga as the basis of Vivekananda Kendra (VK). Ranade ji had been trained in organizational rigour with the RSS and in tune with the emerging trends of popularity of yoga gave a direction to the Vivekananda Kendra in his first pamphlet "Yoga, The Core of Vivekananda Kendra." The ideology of VK is to integrate the individual with society and channelise the energy of organised collective life for productive nation-building work.

The activities carried out nationwide through projects are:

- Over 64 Vidyalayas for tribal and rural children in Arunachal Pradesh, Nagaland, Assam, Andamans, Tamil Nadu and Karnataka, hostels for Vanavasi Children, 150 Balwadis all over India, non-formal schools for preservation of Vedic Vidyas, personality Development Camps for children, youth camps to motivate them to lead a purposeful life, cultural Examinations to increase the awareness in students about the greatness as well as relevance of Indian culture, non-formal Education through Audio-visuals.

- Matru Sammelan and Women Awareness Camps for tribal women to motivate them to lead a life of purpose, Health care camps including eye check up and operation.
- Deep Pooja and Shiva pooja, Residential Yoga Shibirs of 15 days duration. Residential Spiritual Retreats of seven days' duration.
- Vocational Training in Assam, Arunachal Pradesh, Karnataka and Tamil Nadu.
- Amrita Surabhi Daily offering of handful rice by women, which is collected to feed around 12,000 poor rural children.
- Promotion of use of natural resources like biogas, building materials, herbal medicines. Seminar, workshops and symposiums to create awareness in ecology.
- Training masons, farmers etc., in appropriate rural technology.
- Seminars and symposiums on traditions of Vanavasi communities for their protection and promotion.
- Inter-civilization dialogue and understanding in perspective of Hindu civilization, research and documentation of traditional customs and rituals of Vanvasi communities.
- Publishing thought provoking literature through magazines like Yuva Bharati (English Monthly), Vivekananda Kendra Patrika (English, Thematic Six monthly), Kendra Bharati (Hindi monthly), Vivek Vichar (Marathi, monthly), Vivek Vani (Tamil monthly), Jagriti (Assamiese & English), Vivek Sudha(Gujarati) and many other books also.

Reaching Out to North Eastern States

A splendorous region with a rich cultural heritage, the North-Eastern, in all walks of life, always expressed the great truth of Indian Culture Unity in variety.

But ... The daunting Challenges: Geographical, Demographic, Ideological and Intellectual:

Reaching Out to North Eastern States

- 4,500 km- long international border with Six foreign countries—Bangladesh, Bhutan, Myanmar, Tibet, China and Nepal.
- A mere 22-kilometre land corridor connects it with the rest of India.
- Sparse population.
- The Chinese claim Arunachal Pradesh and of late, Sikkim.
- Indigenous faith and culture under siege due to Infiltration, anti-national and terrorist movements.
- Harmonious traditional inter-community and inter-regional relationships, strained.
- West-centric theories of isolationism and separatism, Westernization in the garb of Modernisation.
- Diversity/Variety misinterpreted as separateness.

Communities of the Northeast, torn by attack on its traditional faith and culture, on its land, on its people, on its way of life, on its family and community bonds needed the healing touch—a healing touch to understand itself, to live purposefully with self respect and self worth; in short, a healing touch to intellectually understand itself as a whole.

Therefore....The Response ...

Vivekananda Kendra Institute of Culture

A Project of Vivekananda Kendra Kanyakumari, the Vivekananda Kendra Institute of Culture (VKIC) was established in 1993 at Guwahati to nurture roots through Seminars, Research, Documentation and publications on the Northeast of India to:

- Understand the richness of our traditional systems.
- Identify the unifying elements that bind us.
- Provide meaningful continuity to these practices in a fast-changing complex lifestyle and
- To be relevant in time – hence Development through Culture.

The Method....

True empowerment: As Prof AC Bhagabati, Former Vice Chancellor Arunachal University [now Rajiv Gandhi University] and Member, Research Council, VKIC, puts its "VKIC combines conventional methods of investigation with participatory research.... People become researchers of their own tradition to identify their own genius. They themselves evolve the methodology for continuity."

Thus far, a total of 212 Seminars, Symposium, guest lectures, research and documentation projects have been taken up by which the whole community is invigorated. **And Hence** ... The VKIC is emerging as the Intellectual Fountainhead of Northeast India, by its very Basic service.

To the communities—That reflects in their (a) initiative for developmental work, (b) protection of family and society bonds—thus enhancing social capital.

VKIC nurtures the roots unseen and the Tree of Development flourishes

Such work has no glamour of service but it is a very basic SEVA because communities regain confidence to move in time, developing through culture.

(https://www.vkic.org/vivekanandakendra.html)

CHAPTER 4

RSS Chronology with Major Indian Political and Social Events

The RSS was begun in tumultuous times, when the nation was in a sense, unsure about its future and was under British rule. From its very humble beginnings with barely a few members, to the all-India organization it became in a short span of time and to the phenomenal growth the RSS has seen despite resistance from government, is remarkable to look back upon.

In this chapter, a chronology of key events related to RSS right since its founding is listed below:[1]

1925 -1930

1925: Doctor Keshav Baliram Hedgewar (Doctorji), the founder of Sangh announced on Vijayadashami day September 27, 1925, that "We are inaugurating Sangh today." "All of us must train ourselves physically, intellectually and in every way so as to be capable of achieving our cherished goal." Formal beginning of Sangh took place in Doctor Hedgewar's house in 'Sukravari' in Nagpur. Training in drill, march etc. was imparted on Sundays. On Thursdays and Sundays there were discourses on national affairs.

1926: The name 'Rashtriya Swayamsevak Sangh' was selected for Sangh on 17 April 1926, in a meeting called for this purpose at Dr. Hedgewar's house, from a list of four suggested names—

[1]*Primary source: rss.org,* with other inputs.

Jaripatka Mandal, Bharat Uddharak Mandal, Hindu Swayamsevak Sangh, and Rashtriya Swayamsevak Sangh.

On 28 May 1926, daily meetings—Nitya Shakhas—were started at Mohitewada ground in Nagpur. Lathi—'Danda'—was introduced in the Shakha. New commands such as Dakhsa, Aaram—were used for the first time in Shakhas. The tradition of commencing the daily activities with salutation to the Bhagwa Dhwaj and concluding with the prayer—Prarthana—in Hindi and Marathi was instituted. First route march—Patha Sanchalan—was held with 30 Participants

1927: Special training camp with the name O.T.C.—officer's training camp—held in May with 17 Participants - Shiksharthis.

1928: First Guru Dakshina Utsava held with a total contribution—Samarpana—of Rs 84. Shri Vitthalbhai Patel, elder brother of Sardar Patel visited the Mohitewada Shakha in Nagpur. March 1928—first ceremony of initiation—Pratignya—was conducted. A selected group of 99 Swayamsevaks participated. Nagpur saw 18 Shakhas by year-end.

First winter camp was held. First Route March with band was conducted

Meeting between Doctorji and Shri Subhash Chandra Bose took place in Calcutta.

1929: In a meeting on 9,10 November, 1929, held at Doke Math, Nagpur, Doctorji was designated as chief [Sarsanghachalak], Balaji Huddar as general secretary [Sarkaryavah] and Martandrao Jog as chief trainer [Sarsenapati].

1930: Congress passed a resolution proclaiming complete independence—Purna Swaraj. Doctorji instructed all Shakhas to celebrate 26 January as Independence Day.

Doctorji with several Swayamsevaks participated in Jungle Satyagraha and was jailed. He designated Dr. L.V. Paranjape as Sarasanghchalak before participating in the Satyagraha.

Black cap was introduced as a part of uniform in place of Khaki cap.

1930-35

1931: Doctorji was freed from Jail on 14 February. Doctorji Started Shakha in Benares.

Sri Bhayyaji Dhani introduced Madhav Sadasiva Golwalkar - Shri Guruji to shakha in Benares.

1932: Central Province Government issued orders on December 15 prohibiting government employees from participating in RSS.

1934: The order prohibiting Government employees from participating in RSS was defeated in the legislative assembly.

Gandhiji Visited the winter camp—Hemant Shibir—in Vardha. He offered his salute to Bhagava Dhwaj.

Doctorji with Shri Appaji Joshi met Gandhiji and explained to him about Sangh and its objectives.

Doctorji purchased Reshembhag ground in Nagpur which became the Head Quarters for Sangh activities.

Shri Guruji was designated as secretary—Karyavaha—of Nagpur Shakha.

1935: Doctorji deputed swayamsevaks to spread the message of Sangh in Mahakosal - Central Province.

1940-1950

1940: Veer Savarkar ji visited RSS Prantik Baithak in Pune.

Doctor Shyama Prasada Mukherjee met Doctorji to express his concern over the plight of Hindus in Bengal.

British Government banned the Sangh uniform—ganavesh—and route march.

Sanskrit prayer—Prarthana—was introduced in place of Hindi and Marathi prayer.

Sanskrit instructions—ajnas—introduced in place of English instructions.

Shri Subhas Chandra Bose visited Doctorji on his deathbed on 20 June.

Doctorji passed away on 21 June 1940, at 9.27 am.

Madhav Sadasiva Golwalkar—Shri Guruji—was designated as Second Sarsanghchalak on 3 July 1940

1942: Congress launched 'Quit India' agitation demanding that British leave the country. Several **Sangh workers took active part in it.**

Ramtek 'Nagar karyavah' of RSS, Balashaeb Deshpande was sentenced to death by British Government. Later, this sentence was revoked by the Government.

1946: Muslim League declared 'Direct Action' on August 16. As a result of riots instigated by the call, 5000 Hindus were killed and 15,000 thousand injured in Calcutta.

1947: Congress accepted Partition of India on 3rd June which was a stunning blow to the Hindus, and more so to the Sangh Swayamsevaks. Hindus were killed in huge numbers in Punjab and Bengal. Sangh organized 3000 relief camps.

India achieved independence on 15 August.

Gandhiji addressed a gathering of 500 swayamsevaks in Bhangi colony of Delhi on September 14 and appreciated the work of RSS that he had seenearlier.

Shri Guruji flew to Srinagar on 17th October to advise the Maharaja of Kashmir to accede Kashmir into Bharat.

In Kenya, Swayamsevaks started an organisation with the name, 'Bharatiya Swayamsevak Sangh'.

Organizer and *Panchajanya weeklies* were launched.

1948: *Gandhiji was assassinated on January 30. Sangh expressed its deep condolences. Shri Guruji was arrested on February 1 in Nagpur. Interim Government blamed Sangh for Gandhiji's murder, banned Sangh and arrested 17,000 swayamsevaks on February 4.*

Shri Guruji announced the closure of Sangh shakhas on February 5.

After the failure of talks with government, Swayamsevaks launched satyagraha demanding the removal of the ban on Sangh on 9 December.

1949: Sangh Constitution was drafted.

Government lifted the ban on RSS unconditionally on July 12.

Shri Guruji was released from Jail on July 13. A rousing welcome was given to him all over India during his whirlwind nationwide tour.

Akhil Bharatiya Vidyarthi Parishad—ABVP—was launched for nation building through student power.

1950: India became a Republic on January 26. Shri Guruji instructed swayamsevaks to celebrate this occasion.

In March 1950, the first Akhil Bharatiya Pratinidhi Sabha was held. Bhaiyyaji Dani was elected Sarkaryavah [general secretary].

Vastuhara Sahayata Samiti was started to help Hindu refugees from Pakistan.

Earthquake and floods in Assam—swayamsevaks swung into action for rescue and relief operations.

1952

Cow Protection Movement—Goraksha Andolan—was launched demanding prohibition of cow slaughter in the country. Swayamsevaks collected 1,75,39,813 signatures covering every part of the country from 85,000 cities and villages. All these signatures were presented to The President of India, Dr. Rajendra Prasad, on 8 December.

Vanvasi Kalayan Asharam was begun.

Bharatiya Jansangh was formed by Dr. Shyama Prasad Mukharjee and many Swayamsevaks joined it. (Dr Shyama Prasad Mukherjee passed away suddenly in Kashmir on 23 June).

Shri Guruji participated in the concluding ceremony of 'Abhinav Bharat' an organization which was founded by Swatantraya Veer Savarkar for the freedom of Bharat.

1954-55

Swayamsevaks liberated the Dadra and Nagar Haveli from

Portugese control on 2 August 1954, and handed over the region to Central Government. Swayamsevaks took leading part in the all-party struggle for the liberation of Goa from the Portugese control.

Bharatiya Mazdoor Sangh was founded in 1955.

1962

Indo-China War – The RSS swayamsevaks were actively involved in supporting Indian soldiers and donated blood. (Communist party had asked its workers not to donate blood to the Indian Army during the war).

1963-64

RSS was invited to participate in the Republic Day Parade on 26 January 1963, in Delhi. Dressed in RSS uniform, 3000 swayamsevaks and band participated in this parade on short notice.

Vivekananda Centenary celebrations started. Sangh passed resolution in 1963 to construct a grand memorial for Swami Vivekananda in Kanyakumari.

Vishwa Hindu Parishad was launched in 1964.

1965

Pakistan attacked India. Shri Lal Bahadur Shastri, the then Prime Minister, invited Shri Guruji to attend the All-Leaders Conference in New Delhi. At the conference, Shri Guruji extended complete co-operation on behalf of the Sangh.

Sri Madhukar Dattatreya Deoras—Balasahebji—was elected as General Secretary—Sarkaryavaha—of Sangh.

In Nagpur—Vidarbha Prantik Shibir was attended by more than 5000 Swayamsevaks.

1966

Drought in Bihar. Shri Jayprakash Narayan was impressed with the selfless service of Swayamsevaks in relief operations.

1st Vishwa Hindu Sammelan held at Prayag.

1971-74

1971: Vidarbha-Nagpur Prantik Shibir was held, attended by more than 10000 Swayamsevaks.

War with Pakistan broke out for the third time. Swayamsevaks took active part in helping the armed forces.

1972: Vivekananda Rock Memorial in Kanyakumari was inaugurated by the then President of India, V. V. Giri.

1973: Sri Guruji passed away on June 5. Memoir of Shri Guruji built in front of Dr. Hedgewar Smruti Mandir.

Balasaheb Deoras ji was designated as 3rd Sarsanghchalak on June 6. Madhavrao Muley was elected as Sarkaryavah.

1974: Tri-Centenary Celebrations of coronation of Chatrapati Shivaji Maharaj.

1975

Emergency was imposed in the country by Prime Minister Smt. Indira Gandhi on June 25.

Sangh was banned for the second time on July 4.

Akhil Bharatiya Lok Sangharshana Samiti was launched to fight against Emergency. Balasaheb was arrested. Many Sangh leaders worked underground.

1977

Bharatiya Jana Sangh was merged in newly formed Janata Party which came to power.

Government lifted ban on Sangh on March 22.

Shri Jayprakash Narayan addressed the RSS meeting in Patna on November 3.

Cyclone hit coastal areas of AP in December resulting massive human loss. Swayamsevaks worked in relief operations under adverse conditions. 2,40,000 clothes and 32,000 utensils were distributed.

Sri Rajendra Singh was designated as Saha Sarkaryavaha—Joint General Secretary.

1979

Second VHP Vishwa Sammelan was held. Dalai Lama and many prominent religious leaders all over the world participated.

In August, Machhu dam near Morvi, Gujarat, burst causing floods. Swayamsevaks helped 12,000 families in distress.

1980

Sangh launched mass public contact programme—Jana samparka abhiyan—covering 95,000 villages and 1 crore families.

Janata Party leaders insisted that no RSS member can become a Janata Party member at the same time. Bharatiya Janata Party was formed over this dual membership issue.

1981

Islamic mass conversion was organized of about 800 Hindus in February in Meenakshipuram in Tamil Nadu. Sangh along with other Hindu organisations protested these conversions in Meenakshipuram and other parts of Tamil Nadu, and held an awareness campaign against religious conversions.

Sanskar Bharati was founded.

1984

After the assassination of Smt. Indira Gandhi in October, attacks on Sikhs led to massive human and property loss to Sikhs in Delhi. Hundreds of Sikh families were given protection in Swayamsevaks' homes; relief camps were set up for the needy and necessary service rendered at their homes in Delhi and other parts of the country.

Reconstruction of Golden Temple after Operation Blue-Star. Swayamsevaks in large number participated in the Karseva at Golden Temple in Amritsar.

1985

Sangh completed 60 years. Nation-wide awareness programmes were conducted.

1987

Sheshadriji was elected Sarkaryavah. Sri Balasaheb Deoras, Sarsanghchalak visited Chaitya Bhoomi on 6th December to pay his homage to the memory of late Dr. Ambedkar.

1988

Jana Samparka Abhiyan was launched on the eve of Centenary Celebrations of Dr.Hedgewar. Swayamsevaks contacted 1,50,000 families, conducted 76,000 meetings and collected Rs 11 crore towards Seva Nidhi.

1989

On 25 June the terrorist attack on an RSS Shakha in Moga Town, Punjab, resulted in loss of lives of 18 Swayamsevaks and 6 others. 28 persons were injured.

1990

Karseva was held in Ram Janmabhoomi in Ayodhya on October 30 despite all kinds of restrictions imposed by Mulayam Singh government in Uttar Pradesh.

1992

Babri structure in Ram Janmabhoomi fell on December 6.

Government banned Sangh for the third time on December 10.

1993

Babri Tribunal found the ban on Sangh unjustified and the ban was lifted on June 4.

A.B.Poorva Sainik Seva Parishad was founded.

1994

Prof. Rajendra Singh—Rajju Bhayya—was designated as 4th Sarsangh Chalak of Sangh on March 11.

A.B. Seva Vibhag Started.

Laghu Udyog Bharati was founded.

1996

Sri Balasheb Deoras ji passed away on June 17.

Severe Cyclone hit the Godavari Districts of Andhra Pradesh in November causing 900 deaths and massive property loss. Sangh participated actively in the relief operations under the banner of Jana Sankshema Samiti.

Plane crash in Chakri Dadri, Haryana leaves 350 dead. Sangh's remarkable role in the relief operations were praised by the international press particularly the Gulf press.

2007

150th Year of 1857 was celebrated by Swayamsevaks.

Third World Hindu Conference.

Concluding ceremony of Shri Guruji Janmashatabdi in Delhi. One Crore 60 lakh people, 13,000 saints and 1,80,000 social activists participated in Hindu Sammelans throughout the year.

2009

Respected Sarsanghachalak K.S. Sudershan ji named Dr. Mohan Bhagwat as the next Sarsanghchalak of the Sangh.

Ma. Suresh Bhaiyyaji Joshi elected as the Sarkaryavaha of the Sangh.

'Vishwa Mangal Gau Grama Yatra' was launched by prominent Saints and supported by the Sangh in order to create extensive awareness amongst the people about the importance of cow protection, village centric agriculture.

Signatures of 8.34 crore citizens in support of the cause including those of 75,668 Christians and 10,73,142 Muslims were collected, contact programs in 23,300 villages were held and participated by 11,32,117 people. 201 MPs and 867 MLAs signed in support of the cause. Supporting 'Local Yatras' were conducted at 1,23,796 centers attended by 1,48,46,274 citizens. The Yatra covered a distance of 26000 Km. 9271 full time activists and 141035 others, a total of 150306 participants made the yatra successful. This Yatra was launched on 28 September 2009 from Kurukshetra concluded on 17 January 2010 at Nagpur.

2013

Sangh extended its full pledged support to Swami Vivekananda 150th Birth Anniversary Celebrations that took the message of Swami Vivekananda to the every nook and corner of the country.

In the worst ever natural calamity that hit the Uttarakhand during Char Dhaam Yatra, RSS Swayamsevaks were first to engage in relief activities and actively cooperated the Indian Army in its rescue operations.

2018

The year 2018 can be seen as significant in terms of expanding outreach of the RSS and a move towards more interaction with media.

For the first time, *a three-day lecture series on Bharat of Future* inviting interaction with members of public from all walks of life was held between 17-19 September 2018, in Delhi.

Sarsangchalak Mohan Bhagwat ji underlined the importance of a Hindu identity and unity in diversity with no distinctions based on caste, creed or religion. He said that there can be no Hindutva without Muslims in India. Significantly, despite cordial invitations going out to Communist leader Sitaram Yechury and Congress Party President Rahul Gandhi, they chose not to attend displaying their own lack of tolerance for even listening to another's point of view.

On 19 October 2018 (Vijaya Dashami) annual speech at RSS headquarters in Nagpur, Bhagwat ji said "Mahatma Gandhi, whose 150th birth anniversary is being celebrated, provided the political foundation of truth and non violence to the independence movement of the country. This unique struggle for freedom was an outcome of the continuous enlightenment provided by the very same inclusive culture, based on love and truth, as propounded by several great personalities of this country from time to time."

Shri Bhagwat ji pointed to the dangerous social movements that were engineered by vested interests in the last four years causing mayhem and violence instead of following Constitutional norms. He said: "In this connection, every citizen and politician may remember the famous speech by Hon. Dr. Babasaheb delivered on 25 November 1949 wherein he advocates that without all pervasive fraternity in the society, it is not conceivable for the country to move in the direction of justice, freedom and equality and to attain social democracy along with political and economic democracy. The safety of these democratic values and our independence can be endangered without these. The means we adopted to raise our concerns when we were British subjects may be done away after attaining independence. We need to adopt only Constitutional methods, within the ambit of the democratic discipline."

He also called for the speedy settlement of the Ram Mandir Temple issue underlining that construction of a temple is necessary with regard to the self-esteem of the people. Shri Bhagwat ji said, "it will also pave the way for an atmosphere of goodwill and oneness in the country. This matter of national interest is being obstructed by some fundamentalist elements and forces that play communal politics for selfish gains."

Bhagwat ji said: *"Bharat's progress will have to be achieved by rejuvenating all precincts of national life, being rooted in its eternal ethos.* Whatever is available within the country will have to be rectified, reformed or if necessary, completely discarded as per times and situation; and accepting whatever is noble and useful around the world and adapt them as per the requirements of the country; Both these decisions would be based on the same ethos.

This is the characteristic trait of our nation. This is 'Hindutva.' Any country can progress by being resolute and steadfast on its original character, and not by blind copying.". He stated that foreign British rule and administration were merely overlords of the land and territories. "In the Independent Bharat, our rulers are expected to make the administration people-centric. Political freedom is not complete in itself. All the dimensions of national life have to be reorganized on the basis of 'swa' (self) and self-esteem that inspired us and breathed our life with the sense of 'we the people' during the freedom struggle."

CHAPTER 5

RSS and Independence of India

One of the oft-quoted criticisms is that the RSS did nothing to support India's Independence movement in the 20th century by presenting a false narrative through fabricated history designed to suit the Congress power base in India. Generations of Indians have been taught this and people in the West too might think the same. When, we must never forget that the Indian National Congress (INC), which was the leading national organization advocating for India's Independence from British Rule and could negotiate with the British, was itself started by a British officer (Indian Civil Service), Mr AO Hume, on December 28, 1885; Mrs Annie Besant was one of the strongest advocates of Home Rule and was President of INC in 1917 but the call for freedom did not begin right from the start of INC.

Quick Fact Check

After its formation in 1885, it took the Congress 44 long years to demand complete Independence (Poorna Swarajya) for India in December 1929! Until the 1929 Lahore Session, it had only asked for Dominion Status for India from the British. In his introduction to the fourth annual Report of the Congress, 1888 INC President W. C. Bannerji wrote: *"The principle on which the Indian National Congress is based is that British Rule should be permanent and abiding in India."* Congress President of 1911 Pandit Bishan Narayan Dar had openly called *British Rule in India the "greatest gift of Providence to my race."*

We can thus see why Congress always wanted to demonise true patriots like Veer Savarkar ji, and still does – because he was a firebrand hero who demanded 'Complete Political Independence for India' in 1900 when he was just 17 years old!

The INC was the only organization participating in the organized freedom movement in India as that was what it had been established for. RSS was apolitical from the start, founded by Dr Hedgewar, a staunch nationalist, who was in the INC, and RSS was a cultural organisation. The RSS Pledge (Pratigya) right from its start until Independence used to contain the words "Desh ko Swatantra Kar" ("Free the country"). The RSS pledged to free the country right from the first day of its foundation and encouraged its members to participate in the struggle. *More than half the Swayamsevaks participated in large numbers, were imprisoned, including Dr Hedgewar, and many were killed during the Freedom Movement. But because they participated not as RSS members, they were not identified as such.*

But let us look at the record of the other organizations of the time who are NEVER questioned. In British India, no political group in India actually participated in the freedom movement be it the All India Muslim League, Hindu Mahasabha, Independent Labour Party of Dr Ambdekar or the Communist Party of India. The Communists in fact, did not even support Gandhi ji's non violent movement and saw the INC as a bourgeoisie party.

The RSS was founded by a staunch nationalist Dr Hedgewar, who was a member of INC and from its early days, swayamsevaks were involved in the freedom struggle. With such nationalists on board the RSS, an organization with its very ideology of putting Mother India above everything else, for anyone to claim that that RSS was not involved in the freedom struggle is a huge falsehood.

As Muslim League had already progressed into a party stoking separatism leading to terrible riots and the tragic partition of India, no other organization was seen as pan-Indian especially after the 1930s, but the INC. We must look back to see that after the reins of power in INC, that was founded by the British themselves, shifted from British hands to Gandhi ji and Pandit Jawaharlal Nehru, the nation of India was literally handed over to by the British to the INC on August 15, 1947 after transfer of power. In today's terminology that would be called totalitarian control of a democratic space.

That the RSS did nothing to support the freedom struggle is a well-crafted propaganda to suit the interests of Congress and other vested parties. The thinking of the Sangh with regard to freedom from foreign rule has all along been of a very basic nature. From its inception, the goal before the Sangh was to attain the "Param Vaibhav" (the pinnacle of glory) of the Hindu Rashtra, the freedom from alien rule being just one step in that direction. The transfer of power can at the most be "Swaraj" (one's own rule) but definitely not "Swatantrya" (actualisation of one"s own potential being). The concept of "Param Vaibhav" has ingrained in it the material progress too of the nation, but not by compromising its own identity and interests.

Before this chapter takes the reader through the work of the Sangh during the Independence movement, we must remember that the Sangh always saw the cause before the nation as beyond that of a mere transfer of power. The Sangh had a total commitment to the actualisation of "Swa," in other words the Hindu ethos, and kept itself away from the powers-that-be. After 1947, the Sangh began on its own to extend its influence to varied fields of social life. The Sangh "Pratijna" (pledge), which until then was for the liberation of the Hindu Rashtra, was amended to indicate "Sarvangeena Unnati" (all-round development) of the nation. All social life was planned to be designed on the strong base of Hindu nationalism. Swayamsevaks received training in organisational skill and "samskars" of the Sangh and the determination for national reassertion gradually began to enter one after another field of national life that the Sangh entered. The process commenced as early as in the end of 1940s, and has in later decades encompassed a vast number of areas of society.

Swayamsevaks faced imprisonment and torture under the British but it is after Independence that when most of the Sangh functionaries were unjustly incarcerated, baseless canards against Sangh were let loose by the Congress-led establishment. This underlines that not only was the RSS seen as a threat by the Congress due to its large membership and support base, but every attempt was also made to demonise the organization so that successive generations of educated Indians would look at the RSS with suspicion.

The educational system initiated by Lord Macaulay with the motive of producing an army of "brown-skinned Englishmen," to serve the imperial administration as "the most obedient servants" was another legacy of the British rule in Bharat. True Independence cannot be achieved by a mere transfer of power.

Before Independence too, cultural nationalists in the INC like Pandit Madan Mohan Malaviya, and earlier Shri Lokmanya Tilak, had emphasized on the need for cultural education to ensure the true unity of India. Gandhi ji too believed in this but subsequently INC seemed more eager for the transfer of power than to look into how to build a free nation with confident people. RSS played a crucial role during the crucial few decades before Independence but most of it has been left untaught to Indians.

THE TUMULTUOUS 1920S AND '30S

It is worthwhile to start this section with a quotation from the visionary Veer Savarkar: *"India will never be able to live in peace till a state based on religious fanaticism remains its neighbour."* Anyone reading this could not help but agree. That Savarkar ji could say this in the early 20th century and not now, when nearly everyone would say this, demonstrates his foresight and genuine concern for India. How was it then that the INC did not realize what dangers it was getting India into by Gandhi ji stoking extremist Islamist sentiments in the Khilafat movement, encouraging the Muslim League which was founded in 1907, which initially did not have a separate nation for Muslims on its agenda, but later went on to demand with brutal violence, the vivisection of our beloved Motherland?

Has Anyone Asked if Muslim League Took Part in India's Freedom Struggle?

Everyone knows the Muslim League asked for India to be divided on religious lines. But has anyone asked a legitimate question—because after all, the Muslim League too was born during the Independence movement—if the Muslim League members ever took part in the Freedom Struggle? The answer is, No, they did not.

The All India Muslim League, was formed in 1907 by Sir Syed Ahmed Khan (founder of the predecessor to the Aligarh Muslim University), Sir Khwaja Salimullah and Sir Sultan Muhammad Shah (Aga Khan III) to advance the interests of Muslims in India.

Right from the start, Muslim League was clear that it would work with the blessings and co-operation of the British government, to whom the organisation would always be loyal. Loyalty to the British government took precedence over freedom.

Things turned in the Muslim League only when members saw the British suppression of the Ottoman Caliph in Turkey during World War I as an attack on Muslims as a whole, and then protested, but here too, it was their religion first and not the nation. Mr Mohammed Ali Jinnah was previously a Congressman who later moved to the Muslim League.

The Muslim hatred in India against their own brothers, the Hindus, came out in the form of violent riots and mass murders and rapes of Hindus by Muslims encouraged by the League in the 1920s and '30s. Mr Jinnah, President of Muslim League, finally gave the call for a separate nation for Muslims - Pakistan - and the Call for Direct Action Day - August 16, 1946, where over 5,000 Hindus were massacred in Calcutta in one day, the worst riots seen in British India.

After the establishment of the RSS in 1925, Sarsangchalak Dr Hedgewar told the swayamsewaks that after giving an hour to shakha activities, there is no harm in doing work of any party according to their wish but not using the RSS banner but wearing khadi cap and kurta pyjama as was done by freedom fighters then. In hindsight we can see that the patriotic swayamsevaks were not seen then as RSS members and as usual, the organisation's disinterest in publicity, led to it being easy for people to attack the

RSS later as an organization that did not participate in the freedom movement.

It was Doctor ji's magnanimity, love for India and unity of the people that made him not want to create another political centre through the RSS. All was not well with regard to support for the INC as parties and organizations like the Muslim League, Hindu Mahasabha and Communists disagreed with INC not only on ideology but also on strategy. Doctor ji did not want to create more disunity in those difficult years and believed that the need of the time was to accept the strategy and programmes of the Indian National Congress instead of having separate programmes under different parties.

India was under British rule and Doctor ji knew the RSS had just started so strengthening it was a priority as it could have been finished off by British, Congress and Muslim League. Despite all these concerns, the RSS participated fully in India's freedom movement. The INC was founded in 1885 but asked for *Poorna Swarajya*—Full Independence for India only in December 1929, 44 years after formation of INC! Until the 1929 Lahore Session, its demand was only for Dominion Status for India. And in its initial years, in the 1880s and 1890s, the Congress leaders openly stated that British Rule in India is the Providential Gift to Indians! It took the Congress nearly 20 years to raise a strong foundation even though it had many regional organizations with it. This was in sharp contrast to the RSS which was literally founded from no base at all but grew by the sheer force of character of Doctor ji and the commitment of the selfless team of the initial swayamsevaks.

The RSS Pledge *(Pratigya)* right form its start until Independence used to contain the words "Desh ko Swatantra Kar" ("Free the country"). The RSS pledged to free the country right from the first day of its foundation. It encouraged members to participate in the freedom struggle. Swayamsevaks did so in large numbers, were imprisoned and many were killed.

Even before founding the Sangh, Doctor ji was a patriot right from his school days. In his college days from 1910-16, he was associated with revolutionary movements in Kolkata and then joined the INC on his return to Nagpur *It is not known to many that much before the demand for Full Independence was raised by INC, it was Doctor Hedgewar who was part of a movement in INC which, in fact, made such a resolution.* As a member of INC, Doctor Hedgewar formed the Nagpur National Union with some friends. He was in charge of the volunteer force for the All India Congress Committee session in Nagpur in 1920. It was the Nagpur National Union that submitted a resolution to the Subjects Committee of INC and demanded the Congress declare "complete independence as it sole objective". The resolution (that was rejected by the Steering Committee) added that "It is the aim of the Congress to strive to establish democracy in India and to liberate all nations from the grip of capitalist countries." This was nearly 10 years before INC made the demand of Poorna Swarajya in December 1929!

A few years before the Sangh was founded, Dr Hedgewar was a dedicated participant in the Non-Cooperation Movement led by Gandhi ji in 1920 and was also imprisoned for a year. The fire of patriotism never ebbed in Dr Hedgewar because it was an uncontaminated fire, not tainted by any sense of worshipfulness to the British that had plagued the INC for close to 50 years. This "go soft approach with the British" has been one of the strongest criticisms of the Congress in those days, leading to exits of such great leaders as Sri Aurobindo and Netaji Subhash Chandra Bose, among others. To this day, the Congress tries hard to shake off its shadowy past of being nothing but a British agency and waking up only in the end whereas organizations like RSS were defined right from the start as being for the Motherland and not created to serve any foreign power. It is a shame that the media does not ask enough questions of those days of the history of INC but instead chooses to parrot the Congress and Communist untruths that the RSS did not participate in the Freedom Movement.

Dr Hedgewar (Doctor ji), who had already founded the Sangh in 1925, participated in the 'Satyagraha' against the British Government on the call given to the nation by Gandhi ji in April 1930 after Gandhi ji's historic Dandi March and Salt Satyagraha. After the famous 'Jungle Satyagraha,' Doctorji and others including the next highest official in the newly-founded RSS, Shri Appaji Joshi, were arrested and sentenced by the British to nine months' imprisonment in Akola jail. This was Doctor ji's second time in prison in the Freedom Movement. Here, we should note that these prisons were not the comfortable cosy rooms that were accorded to leaders like Pandit Nehru but were dark, dingy, dirty rooms with no facilities and prisoners faced a lot of suffering.

When Congress adopted the Lahore Resolution on 31 December 1929 demanding "Full Independence" and decided that January 26, 1930, will be observed as Independence Day, Doctor ji was delighted and offered complete support of the RSS, having himself proposed complete independence nearly a decade ago in INC. All RSS shakhas were told to celebrate 26 January 1930, by hoisting the national flag and spreading the message of freedom.

Meanwhile, the British Government was anxious at the growth in the RSS and saw a clear threat due to its strong anti-British government stand and complete support to the Congress. Hence, the Government in Central Provinces issued a circular prohibiting those working in government and local self government bodies from participating in RSS activities. But such was Doctor ji's sphere of influence that it resulted in a huge wave of public opinion against this circular of the British government. Editorials highly critical of the government were published in Maharashtra freedom movement publications like *Kesri* and others. When this issue came up in the Assembly, the government's proposal was defeated. Members of all political parties, including a Muslim Member M S Rehman, defended the RSS. This can be seen as the first attempt by the Government to clamp down on the RSS.

GANDHI JI VISITS RSS CAMP

The unanimous feeling in the 1920s and '30s was that the nation should be free from British rule. RSS, with its firm commitment and brave swayamsevaks, was seen as a strong and united force that was working for India.

Notable Congressmen of that era like Shri Vithalbhai Patel and Pandit Madan Mohan Malviya not only attended RSS functions but seeing the dedication and unity in the organization, also praised it in their speeches. Netaji Subhash Chandra Bose and Dr Syama Prasad Mookerjee visited Dr Hedgewar when he was ailing in 1940.

After visiting a 1500-strong Sangh camp in Wardha on December 25, 1934, Gandhi ji was very impressed by the vision of the RSS and its discipline. He joined Shri Appaji Joshi, who was second in command at the Sangh and also a noted Congress leader from Central Provinces, and offered his Pranam to the Bhagwa Dhwaj. Gandhi ji said he was surprised that the Swayamsevaks did not even know of each other's caste, such was the sense of equality with no reference to untouchability by them. So impressed was Gandhi ji by this visit that he even referred to this 13 years later, when he spoke to the swayamsevaks in Delhi's Bhangi Colony on September 16, 1947, where he said he is convinced that any organization which is inspired by the high ideal of service and self-sacrifice is bound to grow in strength.

THE CRUCIAL 1940S, INDEPENDENCE OF INDIA AND PARTITION

In 1940, the 34-year-old Shri Guruji Golwalkar was given charge as Sarsangchalak by Doctor ji before he passed away. The Second World War had been disturbing the World order in the 1940s and the Indian Freedom Movement was at its peak as was the increasing communalization of Muslims and the demand for a partition of India by Muslim League, a party that was endorsed by the majority of Muslim voters in India.

Guruji also followed the principles laid down by Doctor ji in that Swayamsevaks should take part in the freedom struggle led by

Gandhi ji, again without the RSS banner. He believed firmly in the freedom of India from British rule.

The Quit India Movement was started by Gandhi ji on August 8, 1942, during the Bombay session of the All-India Congress Committee, demanding an end to British Rule of India. This movement was started during World War II and the British were not one to take this lightly. After his famous call to "Do or Die" in the Bombay speech, Gandhi ji and most of the Congress leadership was arrested and imprisoned without trial within a few hours of that speech.

We all know that riots were sparked off across India after the arrest of Gandhi ji which was met with brute force by the British including torture and imprisonment of protestors. And the RSS swayamsevaks were a huge force in this regard, a fact that is never taught to Indians as students. It was the force of the Sangh that was able to galvanise public rebellion at a time when Congress, after the arrest of all its top leaders was left rudderless. In fact, it is well known that Professor Rajendra Singh, also known as 'Rajju Bhaiya' who became the Fourth Sarsangchalak of RSS, had taken part in the Quit India movement in 1942.

Interestingly, there were prominent national leaders of the time who were critics of the Quit India Movement when World War II was raging. One of them was Dr. Ambedkar who said the movement was "both irresponsible and insane, a bankruptcy of statesmanship and a measure to retrieve the Congress prestige that had gone down since the War started." He said it would be madness, to weaken law and order at a time when the barbarians were at the gates."

Parallel Government in Chimur-Ashti – the Unsung Heroes

Even as the swift crackdown on Congress leaders by the British after the launch of Quit India Movement left the party in a weak position, and the lack of leadership was about to make this movement fizzle out, it was the swayamsevaks who kept the fight going and gave their lives for it.

> In the Vidharbha region, in a place called Chimur-Ashti, swayamsevaks were able to set up a parallel government. And the brave Swayamsevaks who showed this courage were executed by the British. On August 16, 1942, at Chimur, many swayamsevaks participated in a Quit India agitation which was ruthlessly brought down by the British. The head of the Chimur RSS branch, Shri Dada Naik, was sentenced to death. Shri Ramdas Rampure, another swayamsevak, was shot dead by the British, while unfurling the tricolor.

In such dangerous times, Guruji, had even before the Quit India Movement, in April 1942, condemned those who were selfishly helping the British Government. He had stated that the Sangh has "resolved to do its duty even if the whole world goes against it," and told the swayamsevaks that that they must be ready to sacrifice their lives for the cause of the country. This was known to the British Government of the time as they were keeping tabs on the Sangh.

But it was not just revolutionary activities, swayamsevaks also provided refuge to many leading Congress leaders such as Shri Jayprakash Narayan and Smt Aruna Asaf Ali, both of whom stayed in the Delhi Sanghchalak Lala Hansraj Gupta's home to be safe from arrest. Smt Aruna Asaf Ali, who was honoured later with the title "Bayalis ki Bijli" ('Lightning of 1942'), in an interview to leading Hindi newspaper 'Hindusthan' in 1967 had said that given that all top Congress leaders were in prison after 8 August 1942, the Quit India Movement had no direction and there were no arrangements to manage activities in the leaders' absence, it will be wrong to say that India got freedom due to the 1942 movement. She said, "After the 1942 movement became directionless after the arrest of the top leaders, I was underground at the house of RSS's Delhi Prant Sanghachalak Lala Hansraj Gupta. He gave me shelter for 10-15 days and made excellent arrangement for my security."

Despite all the restrictions on the Sangh, its swayamsevaks were the bravest of the brave and chose not to buckle under pressure or bow before the British. So rattled was the British government by the drills and training of the Shakhas that on 5 August 1940, the Central Government circulated an ordinance that prohibited drills, use of uniforms and exercises. But this too did not hold back the Sangh and hundreds of swayamsevaks willingly faced arrest.

Guruji wanted complete Independence of India from foreign rule and so recommended reaching out to government employees to campaign with them. He spoke at the RSS Poona Officers Training Camp on 3 May 1942, which was also reported by the British and said, "The Sangh resolved to stand on its own legs, not minding any opposition. It was not possible to get swaraj by begging for it from foreigners and this could only be achieved by strength." Nowhere do we find any mention of any RSS swayamsevak being co-opted or supporting the British in any way during the Freedom struggle.

> Would one rather believe Leftist-history with its falsehoods on RSS *not* participating in India's freedom Struggle or go by official records of the British Government, the colonizers themselves?
>
> What many of us do not know is that the British Intelligence Department in a 1943 report had clearly stated: "The ulterior objective of the RSS is to drive away the British from India and free the country".

In June 1939, the Home Department suggested that the Central Provinces government ban RSS; it had grown to become the strongest organization in CP. However, that ban did not go through as CP's chief secretary Shri GM Trivedi wrote back to the Home Department on 22 May 1940, that it was not feasible as this action would lead to huge protests in the province. The British were nervous about the mass support of the RSS; they knew Sangh was not a party like the Congress that they could manipulate but was an organisation led by a fearless leader in Guruji and swayamsevaks who worked selflessly for the nation. What many of us do not know is that the British Intelligence Department in a 1943 report had clearly stated: "The ulterior objective of the RSS is to drive away the British from India and free the country."

It is pertinent to read of a Home Department official Shri GA Ahmed's noting on a file made on 13 December 1943: "the holding of all camps by any organisation whatever should be prohibited by an order under the Defence of India Rules. This will hit the RSS most, as its main activity is the organisation of camps." Not surprisingly, the Sangh's training camps were raided, literature and arms seized, and organizers arrested.

All of the above (which is only a small part of the evidence that is clearly out in the public domain) shows the dangerous lies that the nation has been fed after Independence, just so that the Congress can retain its one-party control and rule India without any challenge or question.

INDEPENDENCE OF INDIA AND SAVING KASHMIR

India finally achieved Independence on 15 August 1947. It was not an occasion of unadulterated joy for the country but one of immense pain as Congress had supported the Muslim League proposal to partition this great nation of India that had known suffering and foreign enslavement for 1000 years and was finally getting a chance to be free. Pakistan was born on August 14, 1947, and our nation was torn apart with the partition of Punjab on the West, Bengal on the East and allocation of Sindh (where flows the River Sindhu - Indus- the origin of our ancient Hindu civilization, and North West Frontier Province) to Pakistan.

The RSS did not celebrate Independence Day joyously but marked the sorrow and grief of over 10 million Indians who were impacted by Partition—the brutal deaths of 2 million, mostly Hindus and Sikhs, and the forced displacement of millions from their secure homes in West Punjab, Sindh and Bengal. Swayamsevaks had fanned out to refugee camps in Delhi and other cities to help in whatever way they could and the refugees saw that in a chaotic, disturbed and life-threatening time like this, the Sangh was the only support they had.

The period of Independence and the months after were historical, violence ridden and traumatic for Indians. The RSS too saw an unfair ban on it after the tragic assassination of Gandhi ji and the arrest of Guruji Golwalkar for no fault of the organisation. *(Details in chapter—Origin and History of RSS).*

We all know about Independence Day and how the British decided to leave India; so I thought it would be helpful to give the reader some valuable information on the first major war situation that threatened India immediately after Independence—Kashmir. The Kashmir Valley is a raw nerve that still hurts India, is a hotbed of Islamic terrorism that affects global security, and whose roots of mismanagement can be traced to the door of Pandit Nehru and his inept handling of the situation after Maharaja Hari Singh acceded to the Union of India.

Sangh Foiled Muslim League Plan to Assassinate Congress leaders

After the tragic assassination of Gandhi ji on 30 January 1948, Guru ji was arrested, the Sangh banned without any evidence and thousands of swayamsevaks were made to suffer in jail by connecting the RSS to the act of Gandhi ji's assassin, Nathuram Godse. Despite RSS name being cleared of any involvement a year later, this baseless claim of RSS being responsible for Gandhi ji's assassination is still bandied about. But at that very time, a startling revelation was made about how it was the Sangh that actually saved the nation from annihilation after Independence.

How many of us know that had it NOT been for the Sangh, there would have been a mass assassination of Congress leaders after Independence, as planned by the Muslim League, a plan that was successfully foiled by Sangh efforts? Very few know this.

Let us note here that India immediately after Independence was not the country we know today. Partition had happened, millions had died and millions were rendered homeless. Most Princely States had acceded to India but the process of integration with the Indian Union to create a single political entity had not yet happened and the nation was in an extremely sensitive position. Which means that the deadly plan as hatched by the Muslim League, could well have been achieved.

Bharat Ratna Dr Bhagwan Das, a noted Indian philosopher and advocate for freedom, wrote about how the Muslim League planned to kill all prominent Congress leaders in one shot and how it was swayamsevaks who prevented this from happening. Dr Bhagwan Das wrote in an article in *Organiser* on 16 October 1948:

"I know for sure that RSS volunteers have informed Jawahar Lal Nehru and Sardar Patel well in advance about the plan of Muslim League under which the League had planned for armed rebellion and annihilating the Ministers of the Government of India and the senior officers, unfurl the Pakistani flag atop Lal Quilla on 10 September 1947, and establish their government in India.

"Why have I said all this? Had these patriotic and sincere youths not informed Nehru and Patel in time, the entire country today would have become Pakistan; lakhs of Hindus would have been butchered and more than that would have been converted to Islam forcibly and India would have become slave once again. What does it indicate? Clearly, it suggests that our government must utilize the nationalist power of lakhs of RSS swayamsevaks instead of subordinating it".

As the process to enable each of the 550 Princely states of British India to sign an Instrument of Accession and accede to the Indian Union was taken up by the committed and patriotic Sardar Patel, as the first Home Minister of Independent India, there was a problem fermenting in the beautiful valley of Kashmir which was majority Muslim.

It was a very tense process whereby Maharaja Hari Singh finally signed the Instrument of Accession to India on 26 October 1947. In the sensitive period after the Partition of India in August 1947, and the bloodshed on the borders, Sheikh Abdullah, a Kashmiri politician, raised an agitation against the Maharaja asking for an independent country in Kashmir Valley with, naturally, the support of Pakistan.

What's not known by many is that the RSS played a very important role in Kashmir's merger with India. Shri Balraj Madhok ji was the then RSS pracharak in Kashmir, and after listening to Sheikh Abdullah's inflammatory speech in Srinagar in October 1947, he met Sardar Patel, Maharaja Hari Singh, Pandit Nehru and many others and passed on this vital information to them. Maharaja

Hari Singh had appointed a Prime Minister, Shri Ramchandra Kak some days before Independence.

It is well known that Maharaja Hari Singh was in a tight spot. Being a nationalist, he was did not wish to accede to Pakistan. But his PM, Shri Kak, supported Independence like Sheikh Abdullah. There were other pro-Independence kingdoms at the time in India like Bhopal and Hyderabad, and Shri Kak was in close touch with them. But Kashmir also had a Hindu population and Shri Kak knew Shri Madhok ji's was influential among them. He invited Madhok ji for a meeting and tried to convince him that Kashmir should be an independent country. But Madhok ji's asked him if he really believed Kashmir could stand independent on its own, and whether this action of his would not give a fillip to other kingdoms like Hyderabad and Bhopal for independence.

Madhok ji was decisive and just a few days before Partition, gave a report of this meeting with Shri Kak to Maharaja Hari Singh. As a result, the Maharaja dismissed Shri Kak on 10 August 1947, and requested Sardar Patel for Justice Mehar Chand Mahajan, judge of the Lahore High Court, to take over as the Prime Minister of J&K. Shri Mahajan had pleaded the case of Hindus before the Radcliffe Boundary Commission between India and Pakistan. Madhok ji then saw that Maharaja Hari Singh was not pro-independence as had been generally propagated by the pro-Independence faction and that he wished his kingdom to join India.

It was on that critical day of 11 October 1947, when Pakistani Raiders attacked Kashmir that the swayamsevaks sprung into action and saved the day. There was bloodshed all around - many civilians on the Indian side were slaughtered and women abducted in large numbers. After that, on a long stretch of the border, there were continuous raids. The vulnerability of J&K was clear as by October 22-23, the entire Jammu-Sialkot border saw such violence and destruction that several border villages were burnt down. In Jammu city, local Muslims became aggressive and started rioting and this led to series of riots. Jammu city did not have troops to defend it and was in a dangerous situation. But the Swayamsevaks there did not run scared. They faced the pro-Pakistani Muslim elements inside Jammu, and fought back their repeated attacks.

In fact, it is believed that a swayamsevak dressed as a Muslim had infiltrated into the Muslim army camp in Srinagar and thereby got detailed plans of the invasion. It might well have been Shri Madhok ji (though not confirmed) who personally informed the Commander of the State Forces in J&K about the Pakistani plan.

At all levels, Sangh was involved in getting J&K on board the Indian Union. The State Sanghachalak Pandit Prem Nath Dogra ji, submitted several memoranda to Maharaja Hari Singh and held many meetings. Likewise, social and political organisations in J&K also passed their own resolutions requesting the Maharaja to accede to India at the earliest. So active were these organizations that telegrams were sent to the Maharaja in thousands from all parts of Kashmir and other neighbouring states. The Sanghachalak of Punjab, Shri Badridasji, too rushed to Srinagar to persuade the Maharaja and he was someone whom the Maharaja respected.

Guruji Golwalkar essayed a prominent role in convincing the Maharaja to accede to India. It was Sardar Patel who was tense about the situation and had requested Guruji to speak with the Maharaja as he knew Guruji enjoyed the Maharaja's trust. Guruji flew to Srinagar on 17 October 1947, explained convincingly to the Maharaja that it was pointless to think of having Kashmir as an independent kingdom and advised him to join India right away. Maharaja said he was ready to sign the Instrument of Accession to India. Guruji returned to New Delhi two days later and informed Sardar Patel that the Maharaja's was ready to accede to India.

When Pakistani raiders suddenly attacked Kashmir on 23 October 1947, Maharaja Hari Singh sent an urgent message to Delhi for help, and agreed to the accession of the State of J&K to India. Kashmir was merged with the Indian Union on 26 October 1947 and after that in immediate response, the Indian Army landed in Srinagar to free Kashmir from the Pakistani raiders. Until the arrival of Indian Army, it was a contingent of swayamsevaks who defended the Srinagar Airport. Among these braves was Shri Madhok ji, who, over the decades, established himself as a strong national leader and became chief of Bharatiya Jana Sangh in 1966-67.

A Helipad Readied Overnight!

After Shri Balraj Madhok ji's death on 02 May 2016, aged 96, the newspaper Business Standard quoting news service IANS, described Shri Madhok ji's role of 1947 in an article titled "Madhok built helipad overnight for Indian troops in 1947" thus:

"Former Bharatiya Jana Sangh president Balraj Madhok, who died here on Monday, was a hardcore nationalist who prepared a helipad overnight when Indian troops landed in Kashmir in 1947...Vagish Issar, who looks after the media affairs of the Rashtriya Swayamsewak Sangh (RSS), said very few people know about Madhok's work in Jammu and Kashmir after partition. Issar quoted Madhok as saying that when Pakistani tribals raided Kashmir in 1947, there was no helipad in his area. To help the Indian forces land there, he along with Kedarnath Sahni—who too later became a prominent Jana Sangh and BJP leader—and Jagdish Abrol prepared the helipad overnight...."

CHAPTER 6

Sangh and Generational Change

If there is one organization that is presented by the Indian media as rigid, with its thinking cast in stone and no potential for flexibility, it is the RSS. It is amusing that the same media can even sing praises for the leaders of noted Islamic jihadi organizations or praise a known anti-national and terrorist sympathizer like Mr Imran Khan, now Prime Minister of Pakistan, as God's gift to humanity, but singularly attack RSS in the name of actions it has not even committed!

Which is why it is only those who have known the Sangh know of its egalitarian ways, the importance given to debates and discussions, no matter how charged, and who know that it is a continuously evolving organization that has grown in keeping with the generations.

"Hindu Rashtra does not mean there's no place for Muslims.
It is not at all so. The day it is said that we don't want Muslims,
it won't be Hindutva."

– Sarsangchalak Shri Bhagwatji
speaking to a packed hall during RSS Lecture Series
in New Delhi, 19 September 2018

When Sarsangchalak Bhagwat ji said these words and when he said that the words of Shri Guruji Golwalkar (who became Sarsangchalak in 1940) in *A Bunch of Thoughts* calling Muslims as "shatru" (enemy), were relevant to the times then, and were not of relevance now and so are not included in recent editions of the book, the media and many politicians and members of the public were stunned. That book does not pertain to Guruji's entire tenure as Sarsangchalak but is from 1940-1965, when India was tragically divided on the demand of Muslims for a separate country called Pakistan and the post-partition trauma of Hindus and Sikhs caused grief to and loss to the nation. But those who know the RSS, were not surprised by Bhagwat ji's comments because they know the RSS as an organization that believes in responding to changing times and arriving at solutions thereof.

RSS Founder Dr Hedgewar was clear in his view that a small British administration was able to rule over a large country like India because Hindus were disunited, lacked valour (*pararkram*) and a civic character. Hence, the focus in the early days was on organizing and uniting Hindus along with training in martial arts and use of weapons. Those were dangerous times and in the run-up to Independence, with the mass attacks called for by Muslim League and the murder of Hindus, this cadre was necessary for the safety of Hindus. Guruji Golwalkar also continued on similar lines with a focus on strengthening the cadre. All along though, the issue of untouchability was not highlighted.

We must remember that in the early 20th Century, India was a casteist society and even top leaders like Gandhi ji did not support inter-caste marriages as he believed in the varna system. The Indian National Congress was started in 1885 and was always seen as an upper caste Hindu party. It was only in 1917 that INC even considered passing a party resolution to prevent the practice of untouchability; here too, Dr Ambdedkar and other leaders felt that it was mere semantics and none of the leaders did any work on the ground to fight against untouchability.

But the RSS, as it grew in strength and due to its non-discriminatory practices, the cadre too reflected a multitude of castes including the scheduled castes and tribes. Always evolving with the times, in May 1974 then Sarsangchalak Deorasji denounced the practice of untouchability saying, "If untouchability is not wrong, nothing in the world is wrong," in one of his landmark speeches in Pune. He exhorted the swayamsevaks to work towards removal of caste based untouchability from Hindu society. Under Seva Bharti, outreach was going on with socio-economically depressed communities and swayamsevaks started schools and vocational training for residents of slums and untouchables. Hindu cultural training was imparted to them. The outreach to untouchables was also highlighted when Deoras ji said in 1985, Hindu unity is the main purpose of RSS and that the organization believes all citizens of India should have a Hindu culture.

EVOLUTION FROM FOCUS ON SHAKHA TO SEWA

RSS was started in 1925 by Dr Keshav Balirao Hedgewar, also called Doctor ji. He was a medical doctor and staunch nationalist and the stirrings of concern within him of the future of Hindus in an atmosphere of belligerent Muslims and the lack of organization among Hindus in the country sparked the idea of RSS. It was begun with just 17 persons in his simple home in Nagpur, Maharashtra. He was the first Sarsangchalak (head of the RSS) and incidentally, also an active Congressman. (The Indian National Congress (INC) party of today is NOT the party it was in the 20th Century and this fact is not known by many. It is important to note that INC was the only representative national party advocating for independence from the British and had a mix of members in it of varying ideologies like socialists, Hindu cultural revivalists and those leaning to the economic right.)

In the early days of the RSS, with increasing separatist activity from Muslims and riots in several areas in India in which thousands of Hindus were brutally murdered, raped and forcibly converted to Islam (like the Moplah riots in Malabar, Kerala), the aim was to organize a Hindu society that had been mostly divided by caste and was unable to withstand the onslaught of the more organized Muslims.

The SHAKHA was the focus, and marked the genius of Dr Hedgewar - as a meeting place where young men at village, district or state level could meet and be trained in the martial arts, gain an understanding of India's Hindu spiritual heritage and the need for freeing India from British rule.

A *shakha* is a daily gathering of swayamsevaks (volunteers) across age groups at a meeting place or ground for an hour. Daily routine programs include physical exercises, singing patriotic songs, holding group discussions on varied range of subjects and a prayer for our motherland. It was these shakhas that enabled the mobilization of hundreds of thousands of swayamsevaks who were able to help millions of refugees from West Punjab and East Bengal who had flooded into India in the horrendous aftermath of Partition and the creation of Pakistan as a nation for Muslims in 1947. The shakha was and is an exceptional brilliant organizational unit as it gave no monetary remuneration to swayamsevaks but gave them all a spirit of such involvement unmatched by any other activity. This is true till today and has no parallel anywhere in the world.

Though Sewa was always a part of RSS, the transition in RSS from a Shakha orientation to the focus on *SEWA* in an organized manner happened over the decades after Independence to address the problems faced by Indians at the grassroots on account of poverty and social discrimination. This generational change was led by Sarsangchalak Shri Balasaheb Deoras ji. Though the RSS swayamsevaks had been doing Sewa in all their activities since inception and the affiliate organizations like Vanvasi Kalyan Ashram and others had been doing remarkable work with tribal communities, there was no formal structure to activities done by RSS and its affiliates. In April 1978, Shri Deoras ji addressed swayamsevaks in large numbers in Delhi, where he asked the swayamsevaks to raise the self-respect of the socio-economically deprived communities of India. He spoke about the need for doing service through a formal structure and this led to starting Seva Bharati that year. Seva Bharti is the official organization under whom are all RSS' and affiliates Sewa-related activities.

This transition itself marks a classic case of evolution in an organization viz. society where it is responsive to people's needs. Affiliate organizations have been constituted as and when a felt need from communities is perceived. These organizations function as independent bodies in themselves. A good example of a neglected community need that the RSS responded to a few years after Independence is the Akhil Bharatiya Vanvasi Kalyan Ashram that was formed in 1952 to serve vulnerable tribals who number an estimated 104 lakh-plus in India today. This affiliate organization was formed to prevent tribal exploitation on economic and hence religious grounds by vested interests especially conversion to religions like Christianity whose missionaries are active in these regions and whose community service is an inducement done to convert the communities to Christianity.

A FLEXIBLE ORGANISATION TILL DATE

> Deoras ji, the third Sarsangchalak from 1973-1994 had, akin to Veer Savarkar's views said: "We do believe in the one-culture and one-nation Hindu rashtra. But our definition of Hindu is not limited to any particular kind of faith. Our definition of Hindu includes those who believe in the one-culture and one-nation theory of this country. They can all form part of the Hindu-rashtra. So by Hindu we do not mean any particular type of faith. We use the word Hindu in a broader sense."

Anyone who claims the RSS is rigid and obscurantist in its ideology is clearly misinformed. As the RSS evolved from Shakha to Sewa, it was the third Sarsangchalak, Deoras ji, an iconic leader who charted a different path for the RSS and differed on some of Guruji Golwalkar's previous views. Deoras ji as third Sarsangchalak publicly denounced untouchability in 1974 and this gave an impetus to swayamsevaks to work sincerely for all Indians. The focus on Sewa for the communities in need led to an increase in the membership of the Sangh and strengthened the organization at national level. Its footprint expanded in South India and North East India in the

1980s. The cohesive functioning of all RSS affiliate organizations with the same apolitical identity of the RSS and committed work with the socio-economically deprived has struck a chord with even the most cynical of Indians.

As the RSS expanded nationwide through Sewa, politically too there was an energy that took shape in response to the need of the time. Again, Deoras ji showed a different mindset by offering RSS support to the JP Movement (named after anti-Indira Gandhi social activist Shri Jayaprakash Narayan). JP led millions of students and activists to fight the blatant misrule of Prime Minister Indira Gandhi in the mid-1970s that had led the nation to rampant corruption by ministers and government employees and economic despair in the nation (this eventually frightened Smt Indira Gandhi into imposing an unjustifiable Emergency across India). Though Shri Jayaprakash Narayan was a staunch socialist, Deoras ji believed in the cause he led as it represented the genuine outrage of the people of India and the RSS supported it. Such flexibility is rare in organizations as most tend to be comfortable in their insular world view.

- The Bharatiya Jan Sangh founded in 1951, was envisoned by the exceptional Dr Shyama Prasad Mukherjee who had served in the first Cabinet of Prime Minister Nehru but fell out with him on policy issues. He, all of a sudden, passed away at the age of 52, in Srinagar, on 23 June 1953. The Jan Sangh had allied with the Janata Party when it came to power in 1977 after defeating Indira Gandhi following the draconian Emergency. But after a fallout with the Janata Party alliance, the Jan Sangh reconstituted itself as the Bharatiya Janata Party in 1980. This too marks a generational change – from Shakha to Sewa to a political party to fulfill the legitimate political aspirations of all nationalistic Indians.
- The RSS in its very origins was not an organization founded by elderly leaders but by a 36-year-old Dr Kesav Baliram Hedgewar ji. Likewise, Shri Guruji Golwalkar was also just 34 years old

when he took over as Sarsangchalak. This was the time when the Muslim demand for Pakistan was gaining ground and was striking at the security of the nation. Many swayamsevaks who participated in the Quit India Movement had been arrested and some were executed by the British. Guruji's views which are always taken as the defining views of the RSS were due to the threat to the existence of India and Hindus at the time. As the decades passed, views of the RSS also changed with the times.

- While top leadership in RSS progressed to 50-plus years subsequently, the leadership at various levels has been younger and in keeping with the communities it represents. Shri Bhagwat ji himself was 59, when he became Sarsangchalak in 2009, and his appointment marks a generational change. He set 75 years as the age limit for officers across the Sangh Parivar. Across the board, there has been a keen interest to attract more young members and leaders. In 2016, the RSS's khaki shorts uniform that had been inspired by that of the British constabulary, was replaced with trousers. Shakha timings were made more flexible, so that office-goers and students could also attend.

CHANGE IS ORGANIC IN THE SANGH

Often people think the RSS is a dictatorial organization with a personality cult of leaders when it is anything but. Change and evolution is organic to the Sangh which believes that new people should come in bringing fresh ideas. Sarsangchalak Bhagwat ji recalls that when he was entrusted with the responsibility of Sarkaryavah, it was very sudden. There were many karyakartas who were senior to him and it looked like there were no serious reasons for a change of responsibility. But Shri Seshadri ji, who was Sarkaryavah then, said that he had held the post for four terms, so there must be a change. This points to the uniqueness of the Sangh in that every individual swayamsevak is important, and it is the organisation's responsibility to take care of them, but the organisation is not personality based.

A significant change has been that in the Shakhas, previously organisational issues used to be the focus but now issues of social importance are gaining centre stage. In an interview to the *Organiser*, Sarsangchalak Shri Bhagwat ji said, "This is not a change, this is a natural expression. Thengadi ji used to call it "progressive unfoldment". In 'Sangh Prarthana' when we say, 'Samartha Bhavatva…", it means increasing the evolutionary strength. Sangh is instrumental in that process. The swayamsevaks are one as a collective whole and at individual level they work as an element of the Sangh and work for the cause with sincerity, dedication and purity. Earlier also it was the same. Then we were few in numbers so our work was not noticed."

Shri Bhagwat ji said that since the inception of RSS, swayamsevaks have been working at rescue and rehabilitation during national calamities. In 1926 itself, swayamsevaks had worked hard to prevent any disorder during the famous religious fair that takes place at Ramtek near Nagpur. Dr Bhagwat said that it is because the swayamsevaks have increased in number that the work is being noticed now while earlier they are fewer in number.

Swayamsevaks are told that communities whom they work with consider the work of the Sangh as pure and true, and so have high expectations, which all who are in RSS should work towards fulfilling. Shri Bhagwat ji narrated an anecdote of Dr Hedgewar ji saying that a person who goes to office on time and returns home after doing his work sincerely, without bothering about what is happening around him, is considered as a straightforward and good person and a gentleman by society. But actually, a gentleman is one who thinks for society and is conscious of what is happening around him. Doctor ji exemplified this in his life. Shri Bhagwat ji said due to the fact that India was under British rule, it was not possible to effectively contribute in social transformation then but now it is possible hence swayamsevaks are able to work on social development issues all across India.

IN SYNC WITH TECHNOLOGY—E SHAKHA AND MORE

The RSS has never been interested in publicity of its work, a distinction that sets it apart from other NGOs. Around a decade ago, RSS cadre realised that Internet technology could be effectively utilized to expand the organisation's scope of work. In 2009, the e-shakha was begun to connect with those interested persons who wanted to join but could not take time out for attending a shakha. A pracharak is online at a fixed time every day like a regular shakha, to provide an opportunity to people across India to interact with him and learn more.

In order to reach out to Information Technology (IT) personnel, RSS holds weekly shakhas instead of daily shakhas so that the professionals can easily take time out for this shakha as against a daily shakha. This is a sign of how the organization responds to needs of the times. Such sessions are operational in Noida, Bengaluru, Hyderabad and Pune. RSS has also been connecting with educational institutions to reach out to school and college students.

Today the RSS has an active website, rss.org with information on the organization making it easy for people to connect with the organization's work. Its affiliate organizations too have well managed websites. RSS office bearers are active on social media (on Twitter @rssorg) and ensure they always maintain decorum in their social media messaging. Sarsangchalak Shri Bhagwat ji in 2017 had said RSS does not support trolling and aggressive behaviour on the Internet as it amounts to "hitting below the belt."

Shri Bhagwat ji believes social media applications are useful instruments and should be used as per their utility but that we should also understand their limitations and side-effects and should not be slaves to technology. He has rightly pointed out in an interview that social media apps can make one egoist and self-centred. "Social media means me, my, mine and I have to express my opinion on each and everything. Even after knowing that my opinion is part of a collective whole, still without waiting for the collective opinion, I post my opinion. Many a times it leads to misunderstandings, sometimes with our own people, and then you have to delete the same. This happens with many people including swayamsevaks. Self-projection has its limited importance at individual level but not at the organisational level." The RSS has its Facebook page and Twitter account, but not of the Sarsangchalak.

Such is the interest among young people who wish to contribute to the work of the RSS that in 2016, a team of 15 young professionals from reputed business schools and engineering colleges was selected to assist the RSS in adopting a "data-driven, analytical approach" aimed at enhancing its outreach. The new initiatives mainly involve using "disciplined, data-driven approach and methodology, and brainstorming sessions analysing case studies. It was reported in the media that a number of initiatives were initiated under the "Six Sigma approach of sanskriti (culture), sanskar (values), swabhiman (pride), swawlamban (self-help), sewa (service) and satya (truth). The 15-member team of professionals was inducted as part-time members for a few months.

The measures rolled out so far include reaching out to college students to draw them towards Sewa. This will help young Indians connect with the concept of nation-building and get involved in working with underprivileged sections of society. As per their preferences and skills, youth are encouraged to work for the nation. The Sangh believes that once young people experience the Sangh and are convinced about its thinking and working, they will automatically become active members and contribute to society.

EXPANDING IN FOREIGN COUNTRIES

It was only natural that the large Hindu diaspora in countries outside India would want to have an organization with the same philosophy and mission that the RSS does. The first *Hindu Swayamsevak Sangh* (HSS) was established in around 1947 in Kenya and is now active in 39 countries with 570 branches. A subsidiary of

RSS, HSS works to support and mobilise Hindus living outside India.

In countries outside India too, the shakha, is the basic unit with the practices followed based on the country it operates in. The US has the second-largest number of shakhas outside India - in 2016, there were 172 shakhas in the US, the largest shakha network outside India. HSS members have strong links with India and contribute to their homeland during national disasters and calamities as well as for developmental work.

In what can be seen as a clear example of generational change, way back in 1953 Guruji Golwalkar, while speaking to Pracharaks from the states, had spoken about overseas Hindus and their philosophical connect with India. He had said then that the RSS had a "World Mission" to propagate the Hindu notion of the world as a single family - *"Vasudheiva Kutumbakam."* (World is One Family)

The start of the HSS was when two *swayamsevaks* who had settled in Kenya in the 1940s started a *shakha*. As they could not use the term "Rashtriya" since they were not in India, they decided to call it Hindu Swayamsevak Sangh. Subsequently, Pracharaks like Shri Bhaurao Deoras ji and others spent some years abroad to develop the organizations there. The British wing of the HSS was established in 1966 and in the US in 1971.

The RSS, unlike what media would like us to believe, does not shy away from any interaction with external agencies. Shri Bhagwat ji spoke to over 50 foreign diplomats in New Delhi in September 2017 at an interactive session where he underlined that Hinduism is a universal philosophy, it is not a religion but a way of life that does not discriminate against anyone and invited them to visit an RSS shakha. Whether in India or outside of it, the RSS has demonstrated its flexibility in adapting to circumstances without diluting its core values.

CHAPTER 7

RSS and Global Challenges

The biggest global challenge we can see all around us, that has nearly invaded the intellectual space of most Western nations as well as India is that of an all pervasive leftist-media and academic bias in universities. It is the persistent, almost unopposed challenge of manipulating public perception through the media and academia.

The process of a gradual takeover of Western Universities by Left-oriented academics began as a result of subtle, below-the-line Soviet influence right since the 1960s. Today, apart from a few American Universities, it is the voice of the Left in the garb of 'liberalism' and 'free thought' that has gained precedence. This has been conveniently tagged along with by the Islamic radical organizations which have succeeded in creating a feeling of guilt among Westerners about any criticism of radical terrorism or terror-affiliated individuals. To the extent that there have been instances of speakers in Harvard and Oxford Universities invited to speak on aspects related to Islamic extremism who have later been prevented from speaking by such promoters of "free speech."

It is a dangerously twisted narrative which is reflected in the international media too which goes soft on genuine concerns like Islamic terrorism and ignores severe human rights violations in Middle Eastern nations but screams about Hindus being rapists after the brutal Nirbhaya rape incident in Delhi of 2012 or that India is a nation of rapists. This sort of news is fed by India's own media, again with the same bias. One does not deny there are issues around women's safety and the BJP government is committed to ensuring the safety of women. But the alarmist media creates a frenzy without caring to mention that viz. population India's average rate of reported rape cases is about 6.3 per 100,000 of the population (National Crime Records Bureau, India, 2016). While UN Crime Trend Statistics 2013 shows that UK has the highest number of rapes (36.44) and the US (35.85).

Media reportage today is seldom about hard facts but more about pushing a pernicious Leftist ideology while snuffing out legitimate coverage of the Right. In India, the favourite target of the media and any Opposition politician looking for publicity is the dignified RSS, that never responds to vitriolic comments and false propaganda but continues with its service to the people. Leading Opposition leader and President of the Indian National Congress, Mr Rahul Gandhi, revels in attacking the Sangh, without presenting any evidence. Such is the baseless hatred all around so-called intelligentsia that in 2017, Belgium-born Indian developmental activist Mr Jean Dreze actually called RSS a threat to India's secular fabric. If Dreze really cared for the development of the marginalized he would have seen the work of the RSS's affiliates where simple, often poor swayamsevaks themselves, practise selfless service for the larger community irrespective of identity, but people like Dreze choose to ignore these facts.

This challenge that the RSS faces is a global one - that of a dangerously biased media and its well-spun narrative of the RSS being a threat to India and secularism. It may be hard for the reader to accept but it is true that the same media does not care to mention more than a line or two about the scandalous corruption in international NGOs working in Asia and Africa with deprived communities.

Biased Media Coverage

When the shocking activities of Missionaries of Charity nuns and workers selling little babies and infants for a price to any available buyer in the Indian state of Jharkhand came out in the news in July 2018, the criminal activity shocked everyone. Indian media paid lip-service to this disturbing news story and the horrific criminal racket that came to light in a Catholic organization, but nowhere did any journalist call Catholic organizations corrupt or say that all Catholics should do some serious soul-searching, etc.

Naturally, the Western media, contrary to the airtime and print space devoted to lambasting India for any single incident of rape, barely mentioned this crime of selling babies that were given to those Catholic nuns by poor parents, who in turn sold the babies like commercial commodities.

IDEOLOGICAL HATRED TO HINDUISM

The evidence all around with regard to representation in the media points to a very clear anti-Hindu bias. But why should there be one? For a Hindu civilization that has never invaded other countries, destroyed societies, raped women and pillaged in the name of conquest, forced religious conversion, a culture that has peacefully lived its way of life as Hindus, why should there be this derision and hatred?

When the Babri Masjid fell in December 1992, the BBC described "Hindu mobs" and such terminology, but did not mention that not one Muslim was killed during the action of the kar sevaks in Ayodhya. In contrast, the Mumbai bomb blasts in 1993, that were an act of revenge as planned by Dawood Ibrahim and others, where a number of Hindus were killed. Till today, the international media is wary of calling an Islamist terror attack as that done by a Muslim but is more than ready to attack Hindus and call them terrorists.

Hinduism is the only major belief system that believes all Gods are one and completely respects other's religions. It is noteworthy that in contrast, the basic tenets of two major world religions, Christianity and Islam, believe only *their* God is the only *true* God and hold others' beliefs in complete scorn and hatred, and in the 21st century still call people who are not of their religion, pagan and the kafir respectively. They believe that either all attempts must be made to 'convert' the disbeliever from their 'sinful' life, or that they should be killed if they resist. Religions that have had such a dark and violent history get no scorn from the international media but

Hindus do! For no fault of theirs. And all this, even as educated Westerners start their mornings with Yoga and Pranayam, with Ayurveda included for good health. Which are all part of Indian Vedic civilization and a glorious heritage that believed then as it does now, in the free flow of knowledge.

It would be fair to say that it is perhaps because RSS represents an organization of Hindus, one that believes in a cultural identity for a nation of majority Hindus that it is seen as a threat. Britain is a Christian country as former Prime Minister Mr David Cameron has often said in his Christmas speech to the nation, US Presidents routinely say "God Bless You and God Bless America," in a clear reference to a Christian God, but nobody has a problem. That's seen as a given, as normal. But the RSS, a humble NGO, which only wants to ensure service to all and work towards ensuring that India's Hindu civilizational heritage remains unharmed, is seen as a danger.

We can see today that there is a bizarre conjoining of previously opposing ideologies such as Islamism and Communism, which in India, clearly plays out in the nefarious politics of pro-Left institutions like the Jawaharlal Nehru University. The "Bharat Tere Tukde Honge" (India will be cut into pieces) sloganeering on the JNU campus premises in 2016 was led by men and women of Communist leanings and pro-Islamist movements in Kashmir. It would be amusing to call them "students" because the frontrunners of this campaign were around 28-29 years old then, completing their further studies, supported by grants given by the University, the money for which is from hard working, tax-paying Indian citizens! These and other "student movements" leave no stone unturned in attacking Hindu customs, despite the fact that all legal reforms post-Independence were only in Hindu Personal Law and were accepted by Hindus. Hindus have been under the ambit of Civil Law with regard to marriage, divorce or property which guarantees equality, while Christians and Muslim laws were left untouched. But when it comes to the rights of 100 million Muslim women, these very "activists" stay silent. Hundreds of Muslim women who have been thrown out of home when their husbands pronounce Triple Talaq have complained over the years, the BJP government has responded to their pleas and the Supreme Court verdict held the practice of Triple Talaq as against the Constitution. But these Muslim women have almost had to fight alone or with little NGO support, and had to brave threats to their lives, as the ideological position of the so-called activists will simply not call out any bias or discrimination in Islam or Christianity.

This is what is being popularly called Islamo-Leftism and can be seen in several Western countries as well as India. As the Left has lost its mass support base over the decades, the adherents of Left-oriented movements see a strong ally in Islamists as they can together create large scale social upheaval. These Leftists have no qualms in allying with a religion that guarantees practically no rights to women, as long as they can protest against capitalism. For Islamists, it is a show of strength against the Establishment in these countries and a move towards ultimately establishing an Islamic state. In India, as we have seen in the last few years, there is a group of Christians too involved in the "Urban Naxal" movement. Their attacks are relentless against the Indian state and Hinduism but not a word is spoken against Christianity.

Such is the fear of "Islamophobia" that most world leaders, social commentators and especially those of Leftist dispensation, never condemn any act of terror or any discrimination that is practiced by Muslims anywhere in the world. A hate crime against anyone is wrong and condemnable but what is worse is the prejudice in classifying such attacks depending on the community. Every single hate crime against Muslims in America, for instance, gets news coverage for days on end but those on others is barely noticed. This might make it appear that Muslims are the most targeted community for hate crimes in the US, but that is not so. Crime statistics in the US for 2017 show that African Americans were the most targeted community, accounting for 23 per cent of all hate crimes reported in major American cities. Jews have consistently been the most targeted religious group in the US with 19 per cent of all hate crimes. Muslims are way below in that list. Between the years 2002 and 2011, for example, there were 1,388 hate crimes committed against American Muslims and 9,198 against American Jews, 25,130 against black Americans. And yet the fear of Islamophobia is so instilled in the West that intellectuals refrain from presenting facts about the religion and identifying problem areas so that solutions can be arrived at to improve community living and gender equity.

Ideological and Institutional Bias Impacts Protection of Unique Knowledge Systems

> It is worthwhile to note that if Indians themselves do not know enough about their unique cultural heritage and knowledge resources, it will be impossible for them to safeguard the ownership of those precious resources or even want to protect them. An education delinked from the ancient scientific and cultural knowledge of India will be disastrous for knowledge systems of the world at large.

In India, a huge challenge which is also a global one, is that of a warped educational system with no roots in the country's distinctive cultural identity. The current educational system in India is an offshoot of Lord Macaulay's thinking of creating "brown sahibs" wherein the disdain for one's own cultural systems, history and scientific research of several thousands of years past is conveniently ignored and scorned. Often half-truths in the name of history are taught and students are not encouraged to search for more information on their own, with recommended Reading Lists of books only by Leftist academicians. This results in the creation of a uniilateral ecosystem with all graduates thinking as one, and unable to understand who they really are or what India really is.

With a preference for urbanites to send their children to Christian English medium schools, the bias against Hinduism is taken forward even further. All the while, the brutal history of

Christianity with its wiping out of Hellenic civilization, the forced conversions of masses of people in Europe, Asia, Africa and Latin America, is conveniently erased. This is why, the Sangh, with its mission of Sewa with no strings attached, is seen as such as a threat, Because the Christian missionaries adopted service as a cunning way to offer educational and medical services to deprived and vulnerable populations and then traded that with the conversion of those innocent people to Christianity. While the Sewa of RSS seeks nothing in return and is true to the Hindu dharma of doing good because it is the right thing to do rather than in return for blessings or converting people to any religion.

The RSS works in an organic fashion and as its popularity increases, to those who are practitioners of foreign religions in India, the RSS is seen as a threat. And since RSS and most Hindus choose not to be aggressive at any and every attack on its philosophy, they are an easy target. Christian Missionaries do use community service but as a tactic to convert unsuspecting local communities and this is why the growth of RSS frightens them.

The believing Christian and Muslim in India is indeed surprised to see the popularity of ancient Hindu practices like Yoga with millions around the world practicing Yoga (30 million in the US alone) and commemorating the same on World Yoga Day, or Ayurveda, whose popularity is increasing in leaps and bounds. All this has been without any marketing or conversion of those who opt to take these practices up but by the sheer evidence of the efficacy of these systems in healing the mind and body that Hindu saints and seers developed over five thousand years.

It is worthwhile to note that if Indians themselves do not know enough about their unique cultural heritage and knowledge resources, it will be impossible for them to safeguard the ownership of those precious resources or even want to protect them. An education delinked from the ancient scientific and cultural knowledge of India will be disastrous for knowledge systems of the world at large. We all know about how India had to fight hard for

Intellectual Property Rights (IPR) for neem, turmeric and basmati. India has not claimed IPR for Yoga though all sorts of Yoga-related products like socks and shoes produced in the US have got patents! Thankfully, under Vajpayee ji's NDA government, the Traditional Knowledge Digital Library (TKDL) was set up in 2001, as a repository of traditional Indian knowledge and as collaboration between Council of Scientific and Industrial Research and Ministry of AYUSH.

THE POWER OF GLOBAL RELIGIONS

Both Islam and Christianity are global religions and not only have large populations of believers worldwide, but also have access to large funds amounting to billions of dollars. The power of the Christian Church extends right up the US government.

For instance, when US-based Christian charity Compassion International, had to shut down its India operations in 2017 due to evidence of carrying out conversion activities under the guise of social service activities, the US State Department expressed its concern to India in March 2017 and sought "fairer process" for foreign NGOs in the country. Any sovereign nation has the right to shut down any organization that has violated the national laws but one can see the influence of such organizations in US government. India responded by saying charities must follow the law. "The whole matter here is a matter of law enforcement and following the laid-down laws of the country," Foreign Ministry Spokesman Mr Gopal Baglay had said in a press conference. Most American and British mainstream media was sympathetic in their coverage to Compassion International and painted the Indian government as "right wing" and nationalistic. But when Britain pulled the plug on state funding for a leading Muslim NGO Muslim Charities Forum in 2015, after it was found that the NGO had links with Hamas and Muslim Brotherhood, the dominant tone of British media was that it was the right thing to do with only a few sentences on that due process was followed. Western media clearly has double standards when it comes to the well being of their own countries and those of other nations.

The wealth of the Christian churches under all denominations as of 2018, is officially $217.8 billion –Catholic Church under the Vatican is worth $140 billion, Church of Jesus Christ of Latter Day Saints (US) is $67 billion, Church of England $7.8 billion, Opus Dei (part of Catholic Church) $2.8 billion. This is excluding the investments of the Vatican Bank; given the global network of the Church it is difficult to estimate its total wealth, but it is clearly in trillions of dollars. Clear information is not available about the wealth estimation of Islam but 2012 estimates put the assets of the Islamic financial industry alone to be at nearly $1.6 trillion. Adherents of both these global religions are spread across the world and have tremendous influence through ownership of leading media organizations including social media in shaping perceptions worldwide. It is a powerful weapon and is being used indiscriminately to cover up serious wrongdoings from these religions while playing up any event or data of their choice to belittle Hinduism and thereby, India.

The sphere of influence of these religions is evident in mainstream English media in India as well, with leading media houses either owned by supporters of the Congress party, other owners belonging to the Christian faith or Leftist in ideology.

ISLAMIC TERRORISM

World over, if there is one topic that all nations are very concerned and disturbed about, it is Islamic terrorism. Fuelled by a rise in extremist Salafist ideology of Saudi Arabia, and with the support of oil money, Islamic terrorists are being successfully recruited in all countries with a sizeable Muslim population. These include highly educated men and women, who are so passionate in their ideology of militant Islam that they do not hesitate in killing innocent men, women and children in cities in the US, UK, France, Belgium, and others. India has been experiencing the dangers of terrorism for much longer than the developed world, as local terror in India has been actively supported by Pakistan.

But such has been the skewed and dangerous narrative of the United Progressive Alliance government led by the Congress party, that the term "Saffron Terror" was coined and presented as a serious threat to humanity by then Home Minister Mr Chidambaram in 2010. There was support from the media too in this regard and it was disturbing to see the manner in which dangerous Islamist terrorism, that needed to be dealt with by every country around the world, was being deviously downplayed with this new terminology of Hindu Terror. In 2013, Home Minister Mr Shinde too spoke about "Hindu terror."

In 2010 itself, RSS Sarsangchalak Shri Bhagwat ji had firmly stated that terrorism and Hindus cannot be related to each other. In 2017 too he had said, "There is only one country left in the world on which you can't put the blame of terrorism and that country is India. Terrorism and Hindus, terrorism and saffron, and terrorism and the Sangh are oxymorons and can never be related to each other." He noted that this was an attempt to weaken the strength of the Hindus in India and at the same time to appease the Muslims.

11 September 2001 (9/11), marked a turning point in how the Western world saw terror, because this was the worst such attack in the US, when the dastardly jihadi terror attack took over 3000 innocent lives. Since then, attacks have increased globally, and no nation can be seen as safe anymore. 26/11 of Mumbai, the horrific terror attack on India, that claimed over 165 lives, including those of foreign nationals, and seriously injured 600 persons, was engineered by Pakistani terrorist organization Lashkar-e-Taiba in collusion with the ISI.

The rise in "Lone Wolf" terror attacks is being seen worldwide in the last few years, and is a challenge for intelligence agencies. Amidst all this, it is a devious agenda of the media and anti-India groups to divert attention from the serious issue of rising Islamic extremism, by instead, propagating the false threat of "Hindu terror." This only helps obfuscate the growing danger of homegrown Islamic terrorism in India. In sum, what this does is render our nation, India, and the world at large, vulnerable to even greater Islamist terrorist attacks than we have seen so far.

All these global challenges point to the need for a stronger Indian identity and confidence within the nation to face them. When India is able to awaken itself about its own unique potential, then it can be a *Vishwa Guru* (Guru of the World). As RSS Sarsangchalak Shri Bhagwat ji said:

> *"To bring our country back on its feet is the goal of RSS. It is not a selfish or parochial motive. There is a need for it. Around the world, humanity has for the past 2,000 years, tried many things for world peace, But they have failed. They need a new roadmap and India will provide that new path for the people. India has been doing so since millenniums."*

CHAPTER 8

RSS and Call for Justice in Ram Janmabhoomi

A STRUGGLE LIKE NOWHERE ELSE IN THE WORLD

Wherever Christians regained power during and after the Crusades-Jihads, they have NOT continued to keep the churches that had been converted into mosques as such. *Cultural restoration of sites of worship* has been going on since centuries and those mosques have gone back to being churches.

For eg, when the Ottomans conquered the Balkans in the 15th century, many churches were converted into mosques. But in the 19th century, many of these converted mosques that were churches such as the Church of Prophet Elijah (Thessaloniki, Greece. Now a UN World Heritage Site) were re-converted into churches and their minarets removed. In fact, when the Christian Balkan states obtained independence from the Ottoman Empire, they destroyed Ottoman mosques. The only three remaining mosques from the Ottoman period in Croatia were converted into Catholic churches.

In August 2018, construction began for a grand Shri Ram Mandir, a temple for Bhagwan Shri Ram, in Ayyuthaya, Thailand—a city outside India that took on the sacred name of Ayodhya where Shri Ram was from, due to the historic veneration of the Thais for Lord Shri Ram. However, in the Lord's own birthplace, Ayodhya, India, the issue of Ram Mandir—the go-ahead for a temple to be built on the original site where Bhagwan Shri Ram was born—is one that sears through India's national narrative even today. When, even on the principle of justice alone, it should have been resolved a long time ago. Shri Ram is a Lord for whom faith rings strong among the people of not just India but South Asia and South East Asia as well. Over one billion human beings are being deprived of their right to pray in a temple where their Lord, Shri Ram was born.

That Lord Shri Ram is deprived of a temple in his birthplace that is to be reconstructed at the site where it was destroyed, is a huge shame. This struggle for a Ram Mandir to be constructed in a country where the majority population is Hindu, is unparalleled anywhere in the world. Can we imagine Christians being unable to reconstruct a Church if the one in the Vatican was destroyed by invaders, with devotees crying for centuries?

It is an undisputed fact that the Shri Ram Mandir existed until its barbaric destruction by the forces of Muslim invader Babur, led by Mir Baqi in 1528 and construction of a mosque Babri Masjid on that sacred site.

Ayodhya was until very recently in a district called Faizabad in Uttar Pradesh, whose name was restored to Ayodhya by the current BJP government in the state. The people of India have always known that a Ram Mandir existed and Hindus worshipped at the temple which was never used as a mosque. Historians of past centuries and British officers have recorded this too. For instance, H.R. Neville, Editor of the *Faizabad District Gazetteer* (1870), wrote that the Janmasthan temple "was destroyed by Babur and replaced by a mosque." He also wrote" The Janmasthan was in Ramkot and marked the birthplace of Rama. In 1528 A.D. Babur came to Ayodhya and halted here for a week. He destroyed the ancient temple and on its site built a mosque, still known as Babur's mosque. The materials of the old structure [i.e., the temple] were largely employed, and many of the columns were in good preservation."

However, since the matter was dragged into court even before the independence of India, it began to take a legal turn with dispute lasting for decades going into facts and data to prove that a Shri Ram temple even existed! The first recorded communal clashes over the site were recorded in 1853. It was in 1859 that the British local administration fenced the site, marking separate areas of worship for

Hindus and Muslims. This was how it remained for about 90 years. After independence, in 1949, idols of Shri Ram were found inside the mosque leading to civil suits from both parties to the dispute. The government locked the gates, saying the matter was sub-judice and declared the area as disputed. The civil suits were filed for ownership of the Plot no 583 of the area. In 1961, a case was filed against forced occupation of the Babri Masjid by placement of idols.

Such has been the Leftist distortion of history that in the very land of Bhagwan Shri Ram's birth, a painful process went on for over a hundred years (matter first went to court in 1883) where Hindus had to prove Shri Ram's existence. Have Christians ever been asked to prove the existence of Jesus Christ? Have Muslims ever been asked for evidence on anything they believe in? Why then is the Hindu put through this trial?

During the series of Crusades and Jihads in Europe and the Balkans between Christians and Muslims between 11th -13th centuries, there was massive destruction of each other's respective sites. When Muslims subjugated Christian areas, apart from forced conversions, they also took over existing churches by putting Islamic style minarets on them and converting them into mosques. Christians too had taken over Greek and Roman temples in Europe and converted them into Churches earlier. This is a clear symbolism of conquest and subjugation and all those invaders who historically attacked other lands have done this. (India has been no exception; thousands of temples were destroyed or mutilated by Muslim invaders and the "ruins" of temples in North India bear testimony to that.)

But wherever Christians regained power during and after the Crusades-Jihads, they have NOT retained the mosques that were originally converted from churches. *Cultural restoration of sites of worship* has been going on since centuries and those mosques have gone back to being churches. For eg, during the Ottoman conquest of the Balkans in the 15th century, many churches were converted into mosques. However, in the 19th century many of these church-mosques such as the Church of Prophet Elijah (Thessaloniki, Greece. Now a UN World Heritage Site), were re-converted into churches and their minarets destroyed. In fact, when the Christian Balkan states obtained independence from the Ottoman Empire, they destroyed Ottoman mosques. The only three remaining mosques from the Ottoman period in Croatia, were also converted into Catholic churches.

There are facts of history and there are many more such examples to show that wherever majority communities regain control over their own territory they ensure restoration of their own culture. It is only Hindus, owing to their non-violent nature, who have been at the receiving end of this huge historical wrong – of not being able to reconstruct a temple for Shri Ram in his birthplace and restore the sacredness of the site that was plundered and destroyed by an Afghan invader.

The RSS has always had a consistent stand on this issue that a Ram Mandir must be built at the site in Ayodhya. Its affiliate bodies have worked hard on the legal front and in mass advocacy for the cause. But nowhere has RSS given the call to destroy any structure. For many in India fed on a diet of biased news, it is easy to see the demolition of the already dilapidated Babri Masjid by kar sevaks in 1992 as an assault on democracy and what not, when only a sensitive heart can see that action as the expression of a hurt and aggrieved Hindu community that has suffered injustices and historical wrongs and was forced to see a monument dedicated to Babur, a mass murderer of Hindus, on the sacred site of Lord Shri Ram. Has any other population anywhere in the world been subject to such hurt and trauma?

BACKGROUND

The matter of the Ram Janmabhoomi-Babri Masjid case is being heard in the Supreme Court and the nation wished that it was heard and decided upon at the earliest so that the cause of justice will be served. This is especially because the Supreme Court's September

27, 2018, judgment upheld the 1994 ruling by the SC that was in a case related to acquisition of land in and around the Babri Masjid and this was seen by all as a positive step towards building the Ram Mandir. The SC observed that a mosque was NOT an essential part of the practice of the religion of Islam and namaz could be offered anywhere, even in the open.

This was the case that since 1994 had been dragging on the dispute for 24 long years. Previously in 2010, the Allahabad High Court had ruled in the Ram Janamabhoomi-Babri Masjid land title case that the Ayodhya site be divided into three parts. All the parties had appealed against the verdict in the Supreme Court. The issue of 1994 ruling came up again when a three-judge bench headed by Chief Justice Dipak Misra was hearing the appeals against the Allahabad High Court's 2010 verdict. The Muslim parties to the title suit said the 1994 ruling prejudiced their claim as mosque was not seen as essential to the offering of namaaz. In the Allahabad High Court verdict, the land under the dome was allocated to the Hindus. The 27 September ruling was in response to the Muslim petitioners who wanted the 1994 ruling to be reconsidered by a five-judge bench but that fell through. The matter is now being heard as a pure land dispute.

All know that historically a Ram Mandir existed at the said site in Ayodhya and yet since 1992, counsel for Hindus had to prove it citing Archaeological Survey of India (ASI) records of excavations that proved mounds and the existence of a temple under the mosque structure. The 2010 judgment of Allahabad High Court noted that that the predating structure was indeed a Hindu religious one.

With court processes dragging on and the Congress government at the Centre showing least interest in resolving this sensitive religious matter, there was a sense of hurt and betrayal among Hindus. It was in the 1980s that the Vishwa Hindu Parishad launched a movement to reclaim the original Ayodhya Ram Mandir site for Hindus and erect a temple for Shri Ram Lalla (baby Ram) as that was the site where He was born. The VHP was established in the mid-1960s by the then RSS Sarsangchalak Guru ji Golwalkar with the objective of being an organization for Hindu religious awakening through distributing literature on Hindu shastras, lectures and devotional singing. But such was the rampant Muslim and minority appeasement, by the Congress government leading to bold conversion activities by Muslims and Christians that the VHP took on a protective stance in order to protect the interests of Hindus.

A chapter on the Ram Janmabhoomi movement would be incomplete without a mention of Shri Ashok Singhal ji, the strongest leader of the VHP, who had taken up the campaign for the Ram Mandir on mission mode. Singhal ji was a full time pracharak in the RSS and became the working president of VHP in 1984, a position he held till 2011. Singhal ji passed away in 2015 at the age of 89, ailing but working up to a month before his passing - he died without seeing his dream fulfilled. The Bharatiya Janata Party that was formed in 1980 from the Jan Sangh took on the mission politically.

In 1986, a district judge ruled that the gates of Babri Masjid complex would be reopened and Hindus would be allowed to worship inside. The then Prime Minister Mr Rajiv Gandhi told the Uttar Pradesh Chief Minister Mr Bir Bahadur Singh to open the locks of the Babri Masjid and allowed religious rites inside the disputed structure. What many don't know is that the first shilanyas (foundation stone) was laid for a future temple adjacent to the Ram Janmabhoomi site in 1989, and two senior Congress leaders (Mr Buta Singh, then Union Home Minister and Mr ND Tiwari, then Chief Minister of Uttar Pradesh), were also present on the occasion. It is a sign of the hypocrisy of parties like the Congress that blame BJP and RSS for "communalizing the Hindu vote and using the Ram Mandir for political gains," when it is the Congress that has swung both ways when it comes to an issue as serious as the Ram Mandir. The RSS and BJP has always kept a clear stand.

Young Dalit Man Laid Foundation Stone of Ram Mandir

To everyone's surprise it was not a Guru whom the VHP had chosen to do the Shilanyas of the Ram Mandir but a Dalit man from Saharasa in Bihar. Kameshwar Chaupal laid the foundation stone of the Ram Mandir in Ayodhya on 9 November 1989.

Kameshwar Chaupal belongs to a village in Supaul district in Bihar's Mithila region. Mithila is where Devi Sita, Shri Ram's wife, was from. Chaupal recalled in media reports that people there believed Shri Ram was their relative and during marriage songs, the groom and bride would be referred to as Ram and Sita respectively. Like many areas in Bihar, here too there was caste discrimination but it was Chaupal's interaction with a school teacher who was an RSS swayamsewak that changed his life. The teacher helped him get through to college and Chaupal himself then joined the RSS.

Chaupal is now 62 years old. In his childhood, Chaupal was fined because he dared to pray in a temple where his entry was banned. But he has seen a wȯrld of change since then and credits the selfless sewa of the RSS for it.

TURNING POINT

The mass movement for construction of a Ram Mandir that gained momentum in the 1990s can be seen as the largest public campaign in India's history surpassing even those during the freedom struggle. It was a long pending demand for justice that had struck a chord across the nation.

The movement for Ram Mandir was growing stronger by the late 1980s. One of BJP's tallest leaders and Party President L.K. Advani ji began an all-India "rath yatra" (chariot procession) to Ayodhya in September 1990 to galvanise the movement. The government of Bihar under Chief Minister Laloo Prasad Yadav arrested Shri Advani ji even though there had been no violence. It is believed that seeing the masses turn up in even larger numbers than they ever did for then Prime Minister V.P. Singh was the reason for Advani ji's unfair arrest. Despite these restrictions, a large number of kar sevaks reached Ayodhya and tried to enter Babri Masjid complex. But they were stopped by the Uttar Pradesh police and paramilitary forces, resulting in shooting and the unfortunate killing of 16 unarmed *kar sevaks* (this is the figure as per the state government's official records but many believe the actual number was much higher.

On 6 December 1992, the VHP and other affiliates organised a rally involving 150,000 kar sevaks from all over India at the site of the mosque, and it was demolished. Though the biased media tried to show this action as violent, it is important to note that the sevaks did not harm or hurt anyone and violence that ensued later was not perpetrated by them.

Kar sevaks recall that it was a wave that was unprecedented with sevaks bringing down walls with their bare shoulders. Even if warned that a wall might fall on them and it would be better to run away, the kar sevaks did not care. It was a defining moment for them, a historic fight for their Lord that they needed to be a part of.

That date marked a turning point in the mission to build a Ram Mandir in Ayodhya, as a call for justice to the sentiments of peaceful Hindus who had been aggrieved for 800 years and let down since Independence. Sadly, we saw that on the name of the Babri Masjid, instead of Muslim organizations expressing a desire to arrive at a solution and maintain harmony with their Hindu brothers and build the Ram Mandir, they decided to use that as an excuse to create disharmony and unleash terror on people through bomb blasts like Bombay Bomb blasts of March 1993. The Bombay Bomb blasts were the first such serial bomb blasts in the world (12 explosions targeting key centres like the Bombay Stock Exchange, Sahar Airport Terminal and others) and the worst bomb attack on Indian soil. It clearly showed the clear hand of the underworld led by Dawood Ibrahim with the support of Pakistani terrorists.

In Ayodhya, the makeshift temple at the site of the erstwhile Babri Masjid saw a terrorist attack in July 2005 and two years later, M. N. Gopal Das, then head of the Ram temple, received threats to his life. The narrative that the pro-Left and Congress media has led many innocent readers to believe is that it is the RSS that is communal, when it is actually the Muslim organisations who continue to whip up a frenzy on this issue instead of choosing to heal the wounds of history.

After all, it was not a demolition that was carried out by Indian Muslims, as RSS Sarsangchalak Shri Mohan Bhagwat ji had said in April 2018, but by an invading outsider who did it. "The Muslim community in India did not destroy the Ram Mandir. Indian nationals can't do such a thing. Foreign forces destroyed temples here to demoralize Indians," Shri Bhagwat ji had said while speaking at a Viraat Hindu Sammelan at Dahanu in Palghar district, Maharashtra.

The RSS Stand

> *"If the Ram Mandir (in Ayodhya) is not rebuilt, the root of our culture will be cut. There is no doubt that the temple will be built at the spot where it was. The Muslim community in India did not destroy the Ram Mandir. Indian nationals can't do such a thing, foreign forces destroyed temples to demoralise Indians. But today, we are independent. We have the right to rebuild whatever was destroyed because these were not just temples but the symbols of our identity."*
>
> – RSS Sarsangchalak Shri Mohan Bhagwat ji

Sarsangchalak Bhagwat ji had in April 2018 said that said it is the nation's responsibility to restore the Ram Mandir and that the nation is ready to fight for it. He firmly stated the view of the RSS on this sensitive issue during the Three-Day Lecture Series in Delhi in September 2018 that a Ram Mandir must be built on the site at the earliest. When he was asked if the Central government should bring in an ordinance for construction of Ram Mandir or if there should be a national discourse on the issue, Shri Bhagwat said neither was he in the government nor is he in the Ram Mandir Nyas (Trust) but he was a *swayamsevak*, and the Sarsanghachalak, and as someone who had participated in the Ram Mandir movement, he wanted an early completion of a grand temple.

"Lord Ram is not only a God for the majority of this country but is also the protector of this country's traditions and its dignity and is also an Imam-e-Hind for many... all sections of Indian society have faith in him ... We are not talking about any Ram Mandir as many such mandirs were demolished... we are talking about the birthplace of Lord Ram and only a Mandir should come up there," Shri Bhagwat ji said. He added that if the Ram Mandir was built, it would resolve contentious issues between Hindus and Muslims. He also said if the issue is resolved through a consensus, it would also stop many from pointing fingers at Muslims. Bhagwat ji pointed out that had the Ram Mandir matter been considered from the point of view of rashtrahit (national interest), it would have been resolved years ago, but the issue remains unresolved as it turned into a political issue. He added that the Opposition parties will never speak against the Ram Mandir.

However, it is important to note that the RSS was not at the forefront of the Ram Mandir Movement in the past. This movement was being led by the Vishwa Hindu Parishad and the Ram Janmabhoomi Nyas, an organization of Hindu saints promoted by VHP. It was in the mid-1980s, when in a meeting with leaders of the organisation from all the states, the then RSS Sarsangchalak Shri Balasaheb Deoras ji had asked: "Should the RSS plunge fully into the Ram Janmabhoomi movement or allow it to be led by the Vishwa Hindu Parishad and the Ram Janmabhoomi Nyas?" The assembled leaders from all over the country unanimously supported the idea of the RSS getting into the movement. Shri Ram Madhav ji recalls the meeting and how assembled leaders were fired by the passion for building the Ram Mandir and they knew it "had to be a movement to the finish," with the conclusion being the construction of a grand Ram Mandir at the site where Shri Ram was born. He pointed out in a column in the Indian Express (6 December 2017) that RSS's decision to join this movement completely transformed the character of the movement from that of a religious one to a movement for national self-respect and honour. For the first time, the BJP adopted a resolution on the Ram Janmabhoomi issue at the meeting of its National Executive in Palampur, Himachal Pradesh, in June 1989. In this resolution, the BJP endorsed the demand for handing over Shri Ram Janmabhoomi to Hindus for the construction of a Ram Temple.

It was the Ram Janmabhoomi movement that galvanized Hindu identity in a way nothing else had before. The Hindu identity was suppressed by a forcefully imposed "secularism" into the Preamble of the Constitution during the Emergency which sought to deny Hindus their rightful space in the public domain and pernicious vote bank politics that saw several political parties create divisions among Indians on the basis of caste and religion. Even non-members of the BJP, intellectuals and writers had written in favour of the Ram Mandir during the 1990s and thereafter and the need to set right a historic wrong. This had become the topic of discussion among educated middle class Hindus too as the realization that they had been denied their rights dawned upon them.

It is important to reiterate that the RSS view is not anti-Muslim. It believes in a strong cultural identity of India based on the civilization's Hindu roots and that all who are Indians, irrespective of the religion their ancestors adopted, are of the same blood and identity. Hence, there should be no discomfort for Muslims to enable the peaceful construction of Ram Mandir in Ayodhya. It is heartening that many sane voices have emerged from the Muslim leadership too who believe that the Ram Mandir must be constructed at the site of Shri Ram's birth place. They have seen through the dangerous politics of the parties that exploit religious differences and wish to make a change. This is a feeling that RSS supports and believes will pave the way for a more peaceful India. However, not all Muslims see through the designs of other parties that use them as vote banks but do precious little for the community's development. It is pertinent to note that in the country of Islam's birth, Saudi Arabia, mosques are routinely brought down to make way for roads and other structures. Only in India, where a Muslim invader chose to flatten a sacred temple to denigrate the Hindus, just as invaders do to conquered people anywhere in the world, has a case of such sentiment for the majority community of Hindus been dragged on for such time and presented to Muslims as a matter of "religious pride" for them.

BJP MP Dr Subramanian Swamy had petitioned for the Hindus' right to pray at the Ram Janmabhoomi, which is what the matter needs to be seen as. He had also for petitioned for daily hearing in the Supreme Court on the Ram Janmbahoomi issue but the case was rejected. Nevertheless, the entire nation knows that this is a critical matter and it is desirable if the Court expedites the process.

It is painful and insulting to Hindus who have historically borne the brunt of Muslim invasions to demand that there should be a mosque and temple at the site where Babri Masjid once stood. Or that there should be a hospital instead of a temple! As has been pointed out in this chapter, nowhere else in the world have the two major religions ever given up claim on structures that was originally theirs when they got back their land. The RSS is clear that only a temple must be built at Ram Janmabhoomi, a grand temple to mark the sacredness of where Lord Shri Ram was born.

It is important for Muslims too to understand that owing to Mr Nehru's and his communist group of "intellectuals", history was airbrushed for all Indians, which prevented them from officially being taught in school that Muslim invaders had committed grave atrocities on Hindus and had destroyed several sacred religious temples, among them the most sacred in Ayodhya, Kashi and Mathura. It is shocking to see educated Muslims get defensive when these facts are pointed out, when instead, if they accept the facts of history and seek to make up for those wrongs that were done in the name of their religion, India would be more united today.

We must note here the immense patience and decency of the Hindu majority population that despite having borne this trauma 600 years ago, the community chooses to follow the law and wait for justice. Indeed, there is no majority community anywhere in the world like the Hindus of India.

Spain's Cordoba Mosque-Cathedral and Catholic Ownership

Not all majority communities in democracies have been as patient or accommodating as the Hindus of India, when it comes to their own religious sentiments.

Spain is a classic example and worth a mention here. The Mosque-Cathedral of Cordoba, a UNESCO World Heritage Site, has seen bitter dispute over its ownership between the state and the Catholic Church. Cordoba is one of Spain's top tourist destinations especially for its grand mosque-cathedral.

Cordoba fell to the Moors in 711 AD and the Cathedral of our Lady of Assumption that existed then was remodeled as a mosque in 786 AD and functioned as a mosque for 400 years. Then the Kingdom of Castile re-conquered Cordoba and the mosque-cathedral began to function only as a Cathedral. While Cordoba was called the most significant Muslim monument in Europe, Spain, a Catholic country, saw its Catholic leadership absolutely not prefer the "mosque-cathedral" description and hence changed it to "Cathedral" in 2010. This was possible because of a change in the building ownership laws in Spain that happened in 2006. Until that year, as the mosque-cathedral's ownership was not clear, the state paid for most of its expenses. The Catholic Church gained control via a legal loophole introduced in 1998 which allows the Church to register title to land as though it were a government body, without having to produce documents proving ownership! If nobody else files a complaint that claim within 10 years, the registration becomes permanent.

The Catholic Church claims its ownership of the Cathedral dates as far back as 1236 with the Christian conquest of Cordoba. The local authorities too are fighting legal battles with the Church with regard to ownership. Mass prayer for Catholics is held in the building, but despite several legal pleas and lobbying by Muslims to pray there, they have not been allowed to by the local Bishop; in 2010 clashes broke out when a group of Muslim visitors knelt to pray. There are activists in Spain who protest the cover-up of the Muslim past of Cordoba by the Church, and the municipal body has won a case but nothing has been done to shake the Church's position on its ownership.

There is significant institutional bias with regard to legitimate Hindu demands for justice and double standards in any argument on the Ram Janmabhoomi issue. Hindus are under constant, unfair pressure to "prove" Shri Ram's existence and provide evidence. While evidence has been amply provided, no other majority religion anywhere else in the world is made to prove its history the way Hindus in India are forced to. Undoubtedly, this has been a matter of tension in Hindu-Muslim relations when it need not be.

In his annual Vijaya Dashami address in Nagpur in October 2018, RSS Sarsangchalak Shri Bhagwat ji re-asserted the importance of the construction of Ram Mandir from the self-esteem point of view, and that the government should pass an appropriate law in this regard if needed.

He said the place of Ram Janmabhoomi is yet to be allocated for the construction of the temple although all kinds of evidence have affirmed that there was a temple at that place. "There is an obvious game-plan of a few elements to stall the judgment by presenting various newer interventions in the judicial process. It is in nobody's interest to test the patience of society without any reason," Bhagwat ji said. He said, "This is an essential task in the national interest."

On 29 October 2018, when the nation waited eagerly for a sign from the Supreme Court that a verdict on the Ram Mandir-Babri Masjid land dispute case would be expedited over the next few months, a three-member SC bench headed by Chief Justice of India Ranjan Gogoi adjourned the hearing to January 2019. The Uttar Pradesh government had requested for an early hearing and media reported that CJI Mr. Gogoi said, "We have our own priorities... whether hearing would take place in January, March or April would be decided by an appropriate Bench."

Appendix

RSS Sarsangchalaks since the Founding of the organization in 1925:

* **Dr Keshav Baliram Hedgewar** – Founder. (1925–1930 and 1931–1940)
* **Shri Laxman Vaman Paranjpe** (1930–1931)
* **Shri Madhav Sadashiv Golwalkar** (1940–1973)
* **Shri Madhukar Dattatraya Deoras** (1973–1994)
* **Shri Rajendra Singh** (1994–2000)
* **Shri K. S. Sudarshan** (2000–2009)
* **Dr Mohan Bhagwat** (2009–present)